SINGAPORE TRA

2023

"Discovering the Cultural Melting Pot of Southeast Asia's Lion City"

BY

Robert C. Patricia

This book aims to give individuals and organizations seeking to boost productivity and efficiency useful techniques and resources. The knowledge presented here is based on in-depth investigation as well as the author's own experiences working in numerous sectors.

The information provided in this book is for informational purposes only and is not intended to be taken as advice from a professional. Any actions taken by readers as a result of the information contained in this book are not the responsibility of the author or publisher.

Despite the fact that every effort has been taken to ensure the correctness of the material presented, neither the author nor the publisher gives any express or implied warranties or assurances on the accuracy or completeness of the contents of this book. All decisions made based on the information in this book are the sole responsibility of the reader.

The contents of this book are subject to change at any time and without prior notification by the author.

TABLE OF CONTENTS

Introduction

Southeast Asian small-island city-state Singapore is renowned for its cleanliness, effective public transportation system, and rich cultural diversity. Singapore, despite its tiny size, is one of the most developed and innovative nations in the world, with a robust economy, a thriving arts scene, and a reputation as a foodie's paradise.

Singapore's cleanliness is arguably one of its most notable features. The city is astonishingly devoid of waste and rubbish as a result of the government's rigorous policies and severe fines for littering. Singapore is an excellent place to live, work, and play since the streets and public areas are kept up, and the air is generally good.

Singapore's superior public transportation system is another factor in its popularity as a travel destination. The island's almost all-encompassing MRT (Mass Rapid

Transit) system is quick, effective, and reasonably priced. This makes it simple for locals and guests to go around and take advantage of everything Singapore has to offer.

Singapore is renowned for having a diverse population and culinary offerings. Chinese, Malay, Indian, and Western cultures are all represented in the city-state, which has given rise to a fusion of culinary styles. In Singapore, you can satisfy your cravings for Chinese dim sum, Malay satay, Indian curries, or Western-style burgers and fries.

Singapore is a center for innovation and technology in addition to its cuisine and transportation. The city-state is home to a strong startup community that constantly tests the limits of what is conceivable with cutting-edge technology. As a result, the city is now lively and modern, with a thriving arts and cultural scene that captures the city's spirit of innovation.

Singapore is a very modern country, yet it also has a rich history and tradition. The architecture, art, and culture of the city-state all reflect its illustrious past. There is no shortage of historical sights and landmarks to see in Singapore, from the classic shophouses of Chinatown to the opulent colonial structures of the Civic District.

The Gardens by the Bay, a vast, futuristic park with towering, tree-like structures dubbed Supertrees, is one of Singapore's most well-known attractions. These enormous buildings are covered with plants and flowers, and at night they light up to produce a breathtaking visual display that should not be missed.

The National Museum of Singapore, the Asian Civilizations Museum, and the Peranakan Museum are just a few of the museums and cultural institutions that can be found in Singapore. For anybody interested in learning more about Singapore's past and present, these institutions are a must-visit. They serve as a display for the city-state's rich history and cultural legacy.

Welcome to Singapore

Welcome to the Southeast Asian country of Singapore, a thriving and dynamic city-state. Singapore is a must-visit location for anybody looking for a distinctive and rewarding travel experience. It is known for its remarkable blend of cultures, immaculate cleanliness, and fantastic gastronomy.

You'll be welcomed by a busy airport that's frequently rated as one of the best in the world as soon as you land in Singapore. From there, you'll have a variety of secure, dependable, and clean transit alternatives to pick from, including the MRT (Mass Rapid Transit) system, buses, and taxis.

The vast variety of cultures that coexist in Singapore is one of the first things you'll notice. A fascinating mingling of customs, languages, and beliefs is produced by the confluence of Malay, Chinese, Indian, and Western influences. Everything about the city, including its architecture and some of the best cuisine in the world, reflects this diversity.

Singapore is a food lover's heaven, to speak of cuisine. There are many wonderful eateries here, from Michelin-starred establishments to street food vendors. The meals that you really must try include chili crab, laksa, and chicken rice. A hawker center is where you should go if you want to have a genuinely one-of-a-kind gastronomic experience because there, you may try a variety of foods from various stalls.

Singapore is renowned not only for its cuisine but also for its amazing shopping. You can discover everything here, whether you're seeking for high-end luxury brands or regional handcrafted things. The primary shopping district is Orchard Road, which is dotted with everything from fancy boutiques to regional clothing companies. Additionally, Haji Lane, a vibrant street lined with independent shops and cafes, is where you should go if you're seeking for something a little more distinctive.

However, Singapore isn't only about eating and shopping. There are a ton of historical and cultural attractions to explore as well. A must-see feature is the recognizable Merlion statue, which is part lion and half fish. You can also go to the Gardens by the Bay, a magnificent botanical area with supertrees that reach great heights and amazing floral arrangements. Visit the Asian Civilizations Museum or the National Museum of Singapore for an insight into the history of the nation.

Singapore differs from other cities in a number of ways, including its dedication to sustainability and cleanliness. There are many parks around the city, including the aforementioned Gardens by the Bay, and the streets are spotless. A vast network of parks, natural preserves, and bike paths make Singapore one of the greenest cities in the world.

The rest of Southeast Asia may be explored well from Singapore. Its strategic location and first-rate transportation options make it simple to travel to neighboring nations like Malaysia, Indonesia, and Thailand.

Culture

A remarkable fusion of customs, religions, and civilizations may be found in Singapore. Singapore has emerged as a global center for commerce, travel, and education. Its rich cultural legacy is an essential component of Singapore's national character.

Trade and migration have played major roles in Singapore's history. Singapore has served as a hub for travelers from all around Asia over the years, including Chinese, Malays, Indians, Arabs, and Europeans. Each tribe contributed its own distinctive practices, beliefs, and customs, which over time merged to produce a rich and varied cultural landscape.

The food in Singapore is one of the most notable parts of the country's culture. The lively blend of Malay, Chinese, Indian, and European flavors and smells that makes up Singaporean cuisine produces a mouthwatering variety of flavors and aromas. Singaporeans take their cuisine very seriously, and the city-state has established itself as a top culinary destination. The foods chicken rice, laksa, satay, and chili crab are a few that you must taste.

The festivals and celebrations in Singaporean culture are another distinctive feature. From Christmas to Deepavali to Hari Raya Aidilfitri, Singapore observes a wide variety of holidays and festivities all year long. These events are distinguished by vibrant décor, ethnic attire, and copious amounts of delectable food. The most well-known of these events is the yearly Singapore Grand Prix, which attracts tens of thousands of visitors from around the globe to see fast Formula One racing right in the middle of the city.

Singapore likewise values family and community very much. With many Singaporean families maintaining intergenerational households, the traditional Asian emphasis on filial piety and respect for elders is still present in Singaporean culture today. Singaporeans are renowned for their warmth and friendliness, and guests to the city are frequently moved by the warmth and generosity of the inhabitants.

Singapore boasts a strong arts and culture scene despite its modest size. The National Museum of Singapore and the Asian Civilizations Museum are just two of the city's top museums. Singapore's top performing arts venue, The Esplanade, presents a wide variety of concerts, musicals, and dance acts all year long. The street art movement in Singapore is also growing, with murals and installations springing up all around the city.

Singapore is a contemporary, global metropolis that hasn't lost sight of its history. With programs like the National legacy Board and the Singapore Tourism Board, the government has made a determined effort to protect and promote Singapore's cultural legacy. These groups seek to promote and maintain Singapore's distinctive fusion of cultures and customs for next generations.

Geography

Singapore is a small island country in Southeast Asia with a distinctive terrain that has been essential to its development both economically and culturally. Singapore may be small, with a total land size of only 728.3 square kilometers, but it has a lot to offer in terms of geographic diversity.

Singapore is mostly an island that lies off the southernmost point of the Malay Peninsula. The island is bordered to the north by the Strait of Johor, to the south by the Singapore Strait, and to the east by the South China Sea. It is connected to Malaysia by two bridges. These waters are essential to Singapore's economy since they are important shipping channels for global trade.

Mangrove forests are one of Singapore's geography's most distinctive characteristics. A large diversity of flora and wildlife may be found in these forests, which are located in the western section of the island. Boardwalks that offer breathtaking views of the forests and nearby waterways are available for visitors to use as they explore the mangroves.

Singapore's coastline is another noteworthy geographical aspect. Despite the island's modest size, there are a surprising number of gorgeous beaches on it, many of which are undiscovered gems just waiting to be found. Singapore's beaches offer something for everyone, whether you're searching for a quiet area to unwind or a location to participate in water sports like kayaking and paddleboarding.

Singapore's landscape has some amazing man-made structures in addition to its natural elements. The Marina Bay Sands complex, which houses a hotel, a shopping center, a casino, as well as the well-known infinity pool on its rooftop, is one of the most recognizable. The complex's location on reclaimed ground is just one illustration of Singapore's creativity in urban planning and construction.

Of course, no geography lesson would be complete without mentioning Singapore's renowned skyline. The famed Merlion monument serves as a symbol of the city's marine heritage, and the soaring skyscrapers of the Central Business District attest to Singapore's prominence as a major international commercial centre.

History

Over 700 years of history may be found in Singapore. The island nation has undergone significant changes throughout the years, evolving from its modest beginnings as a small fishing hamlet to a booming global hub of finance, trade, and tourism. This article will give a succinct history of Singapore, highlighting some of its most significant events and turning points.

Earlier times

The island was known as Temasek in the third century CE, which is when the earliest records of human presence in Singapore were made. The region was a part of the Srivijaya Empire at the time, a strong maritime monarchy that ruled most of Southeast Asia. Temasek was a crucial port for the empire, and the majority of its citizens were traders and fishermen.

Singapore was ruled by the Majapahit Empire, another significant Southeast Asian power, in the fourteenth century. However, Singapore had declined by the 16th century, and the island had essentially been abandoned.

Colonial Period

Early in the 19th century, Singapore started to reemerge as a significant trading center. Its strategic location at the southernmost point of the Malay Peninsula, which made it a perfect port for ships sailing between Europe and Asia, was largely to blame for this. A British nobleman and colonial administrator named Sir Stamford Raffles founded a trading post on the island in 1819, and it soon developed into a booming commercial hub.

Singapore prospered while being a British colony. The city-state developed into a center of trade and commerce, drawing traders from all over the world to its borders. A robust infrastructure, including schools, hospitals, and a contemporary transportation system, was also created by the British on the island. However, there were difficulties throughout the colonial era as well, such as economic downturns, labor unrest, and conflicts amongst the numerous ethnic groups residing in Singapore.

The Second World War and Independence

Singapore was occupied by the Japanese military during World War II. The island was given the new name Syonan-to ("Light of the South") and joined the Greater East Asia Co-Prosperity Sphere, an association of Asian countries headed by Japan. During the occupation, hundreds of Singaporeans were slaughtered or made to work as forced laborers, which was characterized by cruelty and hardship.

After the war, Singapore was once again a British colony, but the island's citizens started to call for more independence and self-government. Lee Kuan Yew's People's Action Party (PAP), a left-leaning political party, won Singapore's first general election in 1959. When Lee became Singapore's first prime minister, the island nation started to progress in the direction of independence.

Singapore's declaration of independence from Malaysia on August 9, 1965, signaled the start of a new era for the city-state. Although the action seemed divisive at the time, it ended up being a great choice. Singapore undertook a program of swift economic development under Lee's direction, changing from an underdeveloped nation to a thriving international center of finance, trade, and tourism.

Singapore today

Today, Singapore is a thriving city-state with a population of over 5 million. The nation is renowned for its high level of life, robust economy, and pristine, natural surroundings. With a highly qualified workforce and a prime location in the middle of Asia, Singapore is a significant player in the world economy.

Singapore will face a variety of difficulties in the years to come, notwithstanding its accomplishments. A few of these include an aging population, an economy that is changing quickly, and persistent hostilities with its neighbors. Singapore is prepared to meet these difficulties and keep on its road of development and wealth because to its strong leadership, creative energy, and entrepreneurial culture.

Architectural Wonders

Southeast Asian island nation of Singapore is home to a number of architectural marvels that highlight the city's contemporary and dynamic nature. These wonders, which include famous skyscrapers and historical structures from the colonial era, showcase Singapore's distinctive fusion of international cultures, customs, and influences.

The Marina Bay Sands is among Singapore's most well-known and iconic buildings. The 57-story, three-tower structure has a huge rooftop infinity pool that views out over the metropolitan skyline. With its 67-meter-long cantilevered design that extends from the main tower, the structure is an engineering marvel. One of the most well-liked tourist attractions in the city, it also has a convention center, a mall, and a casino.

The Esplanade - Theatres on the Bay is another magnificent piece of architecture in Singapore. The distinctive architecture of the structure is modeled after a pair of Southeast Asian tropical fruits called durians. A music hall and a theater are the two main performing spaces at The Esplanade. Additionally, it has a number of food establishments and a rooftop patio with breathtaking views of Marina Bay.

Another stunning architectural wonder in the city is the Singapore Flyer. With a height of 165 meters, the enormous observation wheel offers 360-degree views of the metropolitan skyline. Up to 28 people can fit in each of the 28 air-conditioned capsules, and the voyage lasts about 30 minutes.

A large number of historically significant structures have been conserved and renovated in Singapore. A structure from the colonial era that was formerly a post office is the Fullerton Hotel. Later, it was transformed into a five-star hotel with 400 rooms and suites, an infinity pool on the roof, and a selection of restaurants. The Fullerton Hotel is proof of Singapore's ability to combine traditional elegance with contemporary conveniences.

The National Gallery Singapore is another illustration of Singapore's old architecture. The structure, which formerly housed the Supreme Court and City Hall, has been transformed into a museum that features Southeast Asian and Singaporean art. The museum's design retains the ancient architecture of the structure while incorporating contemporary elements, such a glass canopy that links the two structures and lets natural light into the galleries.

Singapore's Melting Pot

Due to the variety of cultures, faiths, and ethnicities present there, Singapore is frequently referred to as a melting pot. Over 5 million people live in this little island nation in Southeast Asia, with nearly 75% of them being of Chinese heritage, 15% being of Malay descent, and the remaining 10% being a mixture of Indian, Eurasian, and other ethnic groups.

The idea that people from many backgrounds and cultures might come together to form a new, fusion culture is known as the "melting pot" theory. As a result, Singapore has developed a distinctive culture that blends aspects of Chinese, Malay, Indian, and Western civilizations. The food, language, architecture, and customs of Singapore all reflect this blending of cultures.

The gastronomy in Singapore is one of the most obvious manifestations of its multiculturalism. Singapore is renowned for its food markets, or hawker centers, where individuals from all walks of life congregate. These hawker centers serve a wide range of cuisines, including Malay curries, Indian roti prata, Chinese-style noodles, and dumplings. Many of these recipes have been modified to fit regional preferences, creating a flavor fusion that is exclusive to Singapore.

Language is another component of Singapore's cultural melting pot. The four official tongues of Singapore are English, Mandarin Chinese, Malay, and Tamil. A variety of languages are frequently spoken in public settings in Singapore, where many people are multilingual or even bilingual. As a result of this linguistic diversity, "Singlish," a distinctive creole language that blends parts of English, Chinese, Malay, and other languages, has emerged.

Singapore's architecture also reflects the country's multiculturalism. Towering skyscrapers dominate the city-state's skyline, but there are also a lot of old buildings that showcase the nation's varied background. For instance, the Sri Mariamman Temple in Chinatown is a vibrant Hindu temple, while the Sultan Mosque in the Kampong Glam neighborhood is a stunning example of Islamic architecture.

Chapter 1

Planning Your Trip

10 Singapore Top Experiences

Singapore is a thriving city-state that has a wealth of activities to offer to its visitors. Singapore offers something for everyone, from its rich cultural past and cutting-edge skyscrapers to its delectable cuisine and upscale shopping. The following list of the top ten Singaporean experiences will help you create lasting travel memories:

Marina Bay Sands is a posh hotel, casino, and shopping complex that is one of Singapore's most recognizable landmarks. Visitors can dine at one of the various restaurants on the property or enjoy the mesmerizing view of the city from the SkyPark Observation Deck.

Gardens by the Bay: A breathtaking collection of plants and animals, Gardens by the Bay is a must-visit for nature lovers. Visitors may enjoy the beauty of nature in an original and creative way thanks to its spectacular Cloud Forest, Flower Dome, and towering Supertrees.

Sentosa Island: A well-liked vacation spot, Sentosa Island is home to a number of attractions, including the renowned Merlion monument, Adventure Cove Waterpark, and Universal Studios Singapore. Visitors can spend the day having fun and being entertained with their loved ones.

Chinatown: A thriving center of culture, Chinatown provides a window into the history and culture of Singapore. Visitors can stroll through the vibrant shophouses, sample real Chinese food, and browse the teeming street markets for trinkets.

Singapore Zoo: One of the top zoos in the world, Singapore Zoo is home to many different species of animals. By feeding the amiable giraffes or taking the nightly Night Safari trip, visitors can have a unique animal interaction.

A well-known nightlife destination, Clarke Quay is a riverbank neighborhood with hip pubs, eateries, and nightclubs. At one of the various places, guests can take in live musical performances and dance the night away.

Hawker Centers: Singapore's hawker centers are a must-try for foodies as they provide a wide selection of inexpensive and delectable regional dishes. Visitors can sample well-known foods including Laksa, Char Kway Teow, and Hainanese Chicken Rice.

The Singapore Flyer, the biggest observation wheel in Asia, gives visitors a bird's-eye perspective of the city skyline. Visitors can take in the spectacular views while sipping on a cocktail or having a romantic supper.

National Gallery Singapore: The National Gallery Singapore houses more than 8,000 works of art and serves as a showcase for Singapore's art and culture. Explore the galleries to discover more about the diverse cultural traditions of the nation.

Singapore's greatest shopping district is Orchard Road, a shopper's dream. Visitors have the option of shopping at the numerous high-end luxury stores or dining at one of the many hip cafés and restaurants.

First time to Singapore

Singapore is a thriving city-state that welcomes millions of tourists every year from around the globe. The city has something for everyone and is well recognized for its diversity, cuisine, and shopping. There are a few things you should be aware of if you're planning your first vacation to Singapore in order to maximize your enjoyment.

Getting Around

Singapore has a well-developed public transportation infrastructure that makes it simple and economical to move around the city. A quick and dependable subway system that connects practically all areas of the city is called Mass Rapid Transit (MRT). An EZ-Link card, which is a reloadable card that works with all modes of public transit, including buses and trains, is available for purchase.

Singapore is a pedestrian-friendly city with lots of walking pathways and walkways if you want to explore the city on foot. As an alternative, you may hire a bike and tour the city's various parks and scenic paths.

Attractions

Singapore offers a wide range of attractions to suit all interests. The Singapore Zoo, Sentosa Island, Gardens by the Bay, and Marina Bay Sands are a few of the must-see sights. An iconic landmark, Marina Bay Sands features an opulent hotel, a sizable shopping center, and a rooftop infinity pool. A cloud forest, floral dome, and soaring supertrees can be seen at the future Gardens by the Bay. Sentosa Island is a resort island with a variety of activities, such as Adventure Cove Waterpark, S.E.A Aquarium, and Universal Studios. A zoo of international renown, the Singapore Zoo is home to about 2,800 animals from 300 species.

Food

Singapore is a gourmet haven with a wide variety of dining options. The open-air food courts known as hawker centers, which sell a variety of regional cuisine, are well-known across the city. Laksa, chili crab, and Hainanese chicken rice are a few of the specialties you must taste. Singapore features a number of Michelin-starred restaurants that provide a variety of international cuisines if you're searching for a great dining experience.

Shopping

Singapore is a shopping haven that provides a variety of shopping opportunities. The city's main retail district, Orchard Road, is home to numerous high-end malls and exclusive stores. You can find a variety of souvenirs, apparel, and accessories on Bugis Street, a bustling street market, if you're seeking for a more authentic shopping experience.

Culture

Singapore is a multiethnic city-state that holds numerous festivals and events to honor its diversity. Deepavali, Hari Raya Puasa, and Chinese New Year are a few of the significant celebrations. Additionally, the city is home to numerous museums and cultural institutions that highlight Singapore's extensive historical and cultural heritage.

What's New

The cosmopolitan city-state of Singapore is growing and has made progress in a number of economic fields. Singapore has had a number of recent changes that have aided in its growth and transformation. Singapore is now recognized as one of the most innovative and dynamic nations in the world as a result of these developments. We'll talk about some of the most recent changes that have occurred in Singapore in this article.

Technology

For many years now, Singapore has been at the forefront of technological innovation. The nation has made significant investments in building its technological infrastructure, which has stimulated the establishment of numerous technology businesses. The Singaporean government has also developed a number of programs, such as the Startup SG program, to aid these firms. Fintech, biotech, and deep tech entrepreneurs can access funding and mentoring through this initiative.

The creation of the Punggol Digital District is one of the most recent innovations in Singapore's technology industry. This brand-new business park was created to help the development of the digital economy. A research and development center for the creation of new technologies will be located in the business park, which will also be home to various IT enterprises.

Sustainability

Sustainability has long been a priority for Singapore, which has advanced significantly in recent years. The nation has implemented a number of steps to help it reach its lofty carbon footprint reduction goals. The introduction of the Singapore Green Plan 2030 is one of the most recent advances in this field. This strategy, which includes efforts like boosting the use of electric vehicles, cutting waste, and increasing the use of renewable energy, describes Singapore's goal for sustainable development over the coming ten years.

The construction of the Mandai Park Connector is another recent advancement in Singapore's sustainability initiatives. This new 1.6 km trail connects the Mandai neighborhood to the Central Catchment Nature Reserve for bicyclists and pedestrians. The walkway is intended to promote environmentally friendly transportation and provide tourists a chance to take in Singapore's scenic surroundings.

Tourism

Singapore is one of the most popular travel destinations in the world, and the nation has been working hard to entice even more tourists. The opening of the Jewel Changi Airport is one of the most recent changes to the travel industry in Singapore. This is a brand-new mixed-use building at Changi Airport that has a retail, a hotel, and a sizable indoor waterfall. The Jewel has grown to be a well-liked tourism destination for both locals and visitors, and it has garnered numerous accolades for its creative architecture.

The establishment of the Singapore tourist Accelerator is another recent development in Singapore's tourist industry. This is a fresh project with the goal of fostering Singapore's startup tourism industry's expansion. Startups creating novel products and services for the tourism sector can benefit from the accelerator's funding, mentoring, and networking possibilities.

When to go from January to December

Singapore is a well-known travel destination that welcomes millions of tourists every year. For all types of travelers, it is a must-visit location because of its unique cultural and natural offers. To make the most of your trip, it's vital to visit Singapore at the proper time of year because the weather there can be rather erratic. We'll look more closely at the best times to visit Singapore from January to December in this article.

January - March
Singapore's busiest travel period is from January to March, which also happens to be the dry season. This time of year is ideal for outdoor exploration because the weather is typically cool and pleasant. The usual

temperature range is between 23°C to 31°C, with little to no rain and sporadic showers. If you wish to engage in outdoor activities like hiking, cycling, and beach activities, now is the perfect season to visit Singapore.

April -May

A good time to travel to Singapore is from April to May, when the weather is still dry and comfortable. Between 24 and 32 degrees Celsius is the usual temperature range, and the humidity begins to increase. However, this is also the time of year when Singapore occasionally encounters thunderstorms, so it is crucial to be ready for unexpected downpours.

June - July

In Singapore, the rainy season begins in June and lasts through July, when rainfall is at its heaviest. Normal temperatures are between 25 and 31 degrees Celsius, and the humidity is at its highest. However, if you're interested in cultural events like the terrific

Singapore Sale or the Singapore Food Festival, this is also a terrific time to travel.

August-September

Singapore's wet season is still in effect from August to September, but during this time the amount of rain begins to decrease. Normal temperatures are between 25 and 31 degrees Celsius, and humidity levels are still high. If you want to see the National Day Parade in August, this is also a wonderful time to go to Singapore.

October - December

Singapore's wet season comes to an end at this time, and the weather begins to get better. Between 24 and 31 degrees Celsius is the usual temperature range, and the humidity begins to decrease. Given the excellent weather and limited rainfall, this is a fantastic time to get outside and explore.

Due to the Christmas and New Year vacations, December marks the beginning of

Singapore's busiest travel period. The typical temperature range is between 23 and 31 degrees Celsius, and there is little rain. However, this is also the time of year when Singapore occasionally encounters thunderstorms, so it is crucial to be ready for unexpected downpours. As there are many events and activities to take part in, this is a perfect time to travel to Singapore if you want to feel the festive spirit.

In summary, Singapore is a fantastic travel destination all year long, but the ideal time to go will depend on your preferences and interests. Although the dry season, which lasts from January to March, is often the busiest travel period, the climate is warm and ideal for outdoor pursuits. It might be muggy and rainy during the wet season, which lasts from June to September, but it's also a perfect time to take part in festivals and cultural activities. Overall, Singapore has something to offer every visitor, all throughout the year.

Going with kids

An excellent vacation spot for families with kids is Singapore. It is a wonderful area to explore with your children because of its unique culture, delicious food, well-known attractions, and hospitable residents. Here are some suggestions for making the most of your family's trip to Singapore.

Plan your itinerary beforehand and ahead of time. Singapore boasts many family-friendly activities, but it is crucial to schedule your days to prevent fatigue and boredom. Make a list of the locations you absolutely must visit, such as Sentosa Island, Universal Studios, the Singapore Zoo, and the Night Safari, to get started. Additionally, you might want to think about going to the Gardens by the Bay, the S.E.A. Aquarium, and the Jurong Bird Park. Once you have a list of the top attractions, order them according to the interests and ages of your kids.

Next, get ready for the weather. Packing lightweight, breathable clothing for yourself and your kids is vital because Singapore is hot and muggy all year long. For sun protection, don't forget to include sunscreen, hats, and sunglasses. Additionally, it's a good idea to pack ponchos or umbrellas in case of rain, as Singapore is renowned for its sporadic downpours.

Third, think about booking a family-friendly hotel. In Singapore, a lot of hotels provide family-friendly accommodations and features including playgrounds, kids' clubs, and swimming pools. These lodgings are also conveniently situated close to well-liked sites, making it simpler for you to take your kids on a city exploration.

Fourth, investigate the regional cuisine. Singapore is a food lover's heaven, and your kids will love many of the regional specialties. Try the renowned chicken rice, laksa and mee goreng, as well as a variety of sweet delicacies like ice kacang and kaya toast. Take the initiative to explore the many hawker centers and culinary marketplaces the city has to offer.

Fifth, use public transit whenever possible. Singapore offers a first-rate, efficient, and clean public transit system. A terrific method to tour the city with your kids is via MRT or bus. Plus, it is far less expensive than using a private vehicle or a taxi.

Finally, schedule downtime and relaxation. It's important to take pauses and have space to recuperate when traveling with kids because it might be exhausting. Visit some of Singapore's many parks and playgrounds, like the East Coast Park and Botanic Gardens. You may also have a picnic in one of the many parks scattered across the city or take a stroll along the Marina Bay shoreline.

In conclusion, Singapore is a fantastic vacation spot for families. You can make your trip memorable and enjoyable for you and your kids by organizing your itinerary in advance, packing appropriately for the weather, staying in family-friendly lodgings, learning about the local cuisine, utilizing public transportation, and scheduling downtime and relaxation.

Going with pets

There are a few crucial things to take into account before your vacation to Singapore if you're bringing pets. Singapore is a well-liked holiday destination for people from all over the world because of its tidy streets, plenty of green areas, and friendly culture. But there are some particular difficulties that must be resolved when it comes to introducing pets. We'll go over all the information you require about taking pets to Singapore in this article.

Prior to anything else, it's critical to recognize that Singapore has stringent restrictions and guidelines for bringing pets into the nation. This is largely because the island country is rabies-free. As a result, there is a minimum 30-day quarantine requirement for any animals entering Singapore. All pets must undergo this quarantine, which may be carried out either at your home or at a facility that has received official approval.

Before you can bring your pet into Singapore, there are a number of additional conditions that must be satisfied in addition to the quarantine time. These consist of:

- A current import authorization from Singapore's Agri-Food and Veterinary Authority (AVA)

- A legitimate health certificate given by an authorized veterinarian in your country of residence

- Current immunizations and documentation of those immunizations

- Your pet will have a microchip placed for identification.

- Three months is the bare minimum age for cats and dogs.

These criteria are subject to change at any time, so it's always a good idea to check with the AVA before you fly to ensure you have the most recent information.

You'll be able to enjoy all that Singapore has to offer with your furry buddy by your side once you've fulfilled all the requirements and your pet has finished the quarantine period. Thankfully, Singapore is a fairly pet-friendly city with lots of pet-friendly parks, cafes, and activities.

The Botanic Gardens are among the most well-liked places to visit in Singapore that allow pets. With so much open space and walking trails to discover, this sizable park is a terrific spot to take your pet for a stroll. Another well-liked location is East Coast Park, which provides a designated area for dogs to play and interact.

There are several options for pet owners in Singapore when it comes to dining. You can eat with your pet by your side at many cafés and restaurants that feature pet-friendly outdoor dining spaces. The Coastal Settlement and Cafe Melba are two well-liked restaurants that welcome pets.

When you're out and about in Singapore, it's crucial to respect other people and their dogs. Keep your pet on a leash at all times, and pay attention to any signs stating where pets are and are not permitted. And don't forget to clean up after your pet because

Singaporeans take cleanliness very seriously and you risk getting fined if you don't.

Guided Tours & River Cruises

Singapore is a thriving island city-state in Southeast Asia, and two of the most well-liked methods to visit it are guided tours and river cruises. These excursions provide a distinctive viewpoint of Singapore's illustrious past, many cultures, and contemporary skyline. This comprehensive guide will assist you in organizing your upcoming guided tour and river cruise in Singapore.

Guided Tours: With a rich history that stems from its colonial past, Singapore is a melting pot of cultures and traditions. An excellent way to see the city's famous sights and lesser-known gems while learning about its interesting past and rich cultural heritage is to take a guided tour.

In Singapore, some well-liked guided excursions are as follows:

City sightseeing tour: This tour includes stops at well-known sites like Chinatown, Little India, Little Merlion Park, Marina Bay Sands, and Gardens by the Bay. Visits to the Singapore River and the Raffles Hotel will allow you to learn more about Singapore's extensive colonial past.

Food tour: The culinary scene in Singapore is recognized for its diversity, fusing Malay, Chinese, Indian, and Western influences. You may sample regional specialties like Hainanese chicken rice, laksa, and kaya toast while on a cuisine tour.

Cultural tour: Singapore's population is as diverse as its cultural legacy, which draws inspiration from China, India, Malaysia, and other countries. A cultural tour takes you to locations where you may learn about the various religions and cultures, including the

Buddha Tooth Relic Temple, Sri Mariamman Temple, and Thian Hock Keng Temple.

River Cruises: The greatest way to observe Singapore's skyline is from the water, and a river cruise is the ideal method to do it. An enjoyable way to see Singapore's well-known sites, including Marina Bay Sands, the Esplanade, and the Merlion, is on a river cruise.

Here are a few well-liked rivercruises in Singapore:

The Singapore River Cruise: Takes you on a voyage around the Singapore River, passing famous sites like Clarke Quay, Boat Quay, and the Merlion. Depending on your taste, you have the option of taking a day or night cruise.

The Marina Bay Cruise: The Esplanade, and the Gardens by the Bay are all visible from this cruise as it takes you on a panoramic tour of Marina Bay. The city skyline is exquisitely lit up during the night cruise, which is really magnificent.

Sunset Sail: The Sunset Sail is the ideal choice if you're searching for a more opulent experience. On this private yacht tour of Marina Bay, you may indulge in canapes and champagne while taking in the breathtaking views of the setting sun.

What to Eat and Drink in Singapore

Singapore is a cultural melting pot, and this diversity is evident in the cuisine available there. The island country's cuisine culture is flourishing, offering a wide variety of dishes and beverages. Some of the must-try dishes and beverages in Singapore are listed below:

Hainanese Chicken Rice

Singapore's national cuisine is hainanese chicken rice, and with good cause. over a side of cucumber and chili sauce, tender chicken is served over fragrant rice that has been cooked in chicken broth. It's a straightforward but filling dish that can be found in hawker centers, food courts, and upscale eateries.

Laksa: Is a popular dish in Singaporean cooking. It is a fiery coconut curry noodle soup. Rice noodles, chicken or fish, coconut milk, and a variety of herbs and spices are used to make it. Restaurants, cafes, and hawker centers all serve laksa.

Satay

In Singapore, skewered meat cooked over an open flame and eaten with peanut sauce is known as satay. Although pig and beef are also available, chicken satay is the most popular variety.

Char Kway Teow

A stir-fry of flat rice noodles with soy sauce, chile, and other seasonings, along with items like shrimp, bean sprouts, and Chinese sausage, is known as char kway teow. It is a standard in Singapore's food courts and hawker centers.

Bubble Tea

Taiwanese beverage known as bubble tea has become very popular in Singapore. It is a tea-based beverage with chewy tapioca pearls that is sweet and reviving, and you can find it in cafés and bubble tea businesses all across the island.

Kopi

Robusta beans, sugar, and condensed milk are used to make the robust brew known as kopi, which is popular in Singapore. In coffee shops, hawker centers, and food courts, it is typically served hot in tiny cups.

Teh Tarik: Is a sweet milk tea made with condensed milk and black tea leaves. The reason it's called "pulled tea" is because it's repeatedly poured between two containers to achieve a foamy, creamy texture.

Best Cocktail Bars in Singapore

There are several options available for those seeking the greatest drinks in town in the city-state of Singapore, which has a thriving nightlife culture. The following are some of the best cocktail bars in Singapore, whether you're searching for a chic rooftop bar or a quaint speakeasy:

Atlas Bar: This sophisticated bar is well-known for its sizable selection of gins and its Art Deco-inspired decor. In addition to its distinctive gin-based drinks, which are presented in lovely antique glassware, Atlas Bar also serves a variety of traditional cocktails.

Jigger & Pony: Is a cozy bar with a focus on classic cocktails produced with top-quality spirits. It is a part of the Amara

Hotel. The bar's laid-back ambience and the beautifully made cocktails make it the ideal place to spend a casual night out.

Operation Dagger: Is a speakeasy-style pub that is tucked away in a basement on Ann Siang Hill and is renowned for its inventive and creative cocktails. The industrial-chic decor of the bar and its distinctive cocktails combine to create a really memorable experience.

Manhattan Bar: As the "Best Bar in Asia" award winner in 2021, Manhattan Bar is a must-see for lovers of mixed drinks. This bar, which is a part of the Regent Hotel, serves both traditional cocktails and its own unique concoctions that draw inspiration from various New York City eras.

Tippling Club: Serves a variety of inventive cocktails, each with a special twist. A tasting menu is also available in the bar, where customers can sample a variety of cocktails and dishes.

The Other Room: Is a small bar inside the Marriott Hotel that serves both traditional drinks and its own inventive concoctions. The bar's dismal, gloomy ambience and beautifully made cocktails combine to create a really unique experience.

Best Hotel Pools in Singapore

Singapore is a cosmopolitan, opulent city with some of the most magnificent hotel pools on the planet. Infinity pools with views of the city skyline and tranquil lagoon-style pools surrounded by lush vegetation are just a couple of the breathtaking aquatic experiences available in Singapore. You won't want to miss any of these top hotel pools in Singapore.

The 57th floor of the Marina Bay Sands Hotel is home to the famous Infinity Pool, which provides stunning views of Singapore's skyline. The experience is extraordinary since the infinity pool seems to go on forever. Although this pool is only available to hotel guests, it is absolutely worth the stay for the pool alone.

The Fullerton Bay Hotel's rooftop infinity pool gives a stunning view of Marina Bay and is located in the center of the city. With a glass mosaic bottom that creates the appearance of a shimmering ocean, the pool has a distinctive design.

The pool at the Shangri-La Hotel Singapore is a lagoon-style pool surrounded by soaring trees and cascading waterfalls on 15 acres of lush tropical vegetation. The pool is ideal for a leisurely swim or for relaxing in one of the cabanas by the pool.

Pool at Capella Singapore: With a cascading water feature and rich landscaping, the pool at Capella Singapore provides a picture-perfect backdrop. Swimmers can unwind and relax while taking in the surrounding natural splendor.

Three distinct pools, a water slide, and a kiddie pool are all part of the expansive pool complex at the opulent Sofitel Singapore Sentosa Resort & Spa. Families and couples searching for a fun and relaxing weekend will love the resort.

Outdoor Adventures in Singapore

Singapore is known for its busy urban environment, but the city-state is also home to a number of thrilling outdoor activities that will make your heart race. There are plenty of thrilling activities to try, from lush rainforests to sandy beaches.

Hiking is a well-liked outdoor activity in Singapore. Despite the city-state's tiny size, it is home to a number of nature reserves, including MacRitchie Reservoir Park and

Bukit Timah Nature Reserve. These parks provide a selection of hiking paths for hikers of all experience levels. There are activities for everyone, ranging from leisurely strolls to strenuous treks. You may appreciate Singapore's natural beauty and get a different perspective on the city by hiking in these parks.

Water sports are another outdoor activity you may try in Singapore. The city-state is surrounded by water, making it the ideal location to try water sports like wakeboarding, kayaking, and stand-up paddleboarding. You may try these activities and more at the beaches and water sports facilities on Sentosa Island.

At AJ Hackett Sentosa, you can try bungee jumping if you're seeking for a rush. Jumping while being held by a bungee cord from a high platform is what this pastime entails. Although it's not for the faint of heart, you'll definitely feel an adrenaline rush.

Cycling is a terrific method to see Singapore if you like to move more slowly. The city-state boasts a vast network of bike lanes, which includes the well-known East Coast Park. You can hire a bike and spend the day cycling about the city.

Finally, give the Night Safari a try if you're searching for a distinctive outdoor experience. This recognized attraction transports visitors on a tram ride through a park where they may get up close and personal with nocturnal creatures. It's an exhilarating experience that is unmatched in Singapore.

Chapter 2

Transport

Arriving in Singapore

Changi Airport

Any traveler's experience arriving in Singapore via Changi Airport has the potential to be life-changing. Changi Airport, one of the busiest airports in the world, is renowned for its first-rate amenities, effective management, and friendly environment.

As soon as you get off the plane, Singapore will welcome you with its kind and helpful hospitality. A variety of services are available at Changi Airport to make it easier for visitors to get about the airport and the city. The airport staff is available to help with any queries or problems you may have regarding everything from luggage handling to customs clearance.

The magnificent architecture of Changi Airport is among its most outstanding features. The airport has a number of lovely plants and installations that give the building a resort-like atmosphere. For instance, the Butterfly Garden is a stunning refuge with more than a thousand butterflies and unusual flora. Other well-liked destinations that provide a calm respite from the commotion of travel include the Sunflower Garden and the Cactus Garden.

Travelers can find a variety of dining and shopping options at Changi Airport. There is something for everyone, from upscale boutiques to cheap street cuisine. In fact, the airport has a superb food culture, offering everything from Michelin-starred restaurants to neighborhood hawker shops.

Changi Airport also provides a range of entertainment alternatives for individuals who have a lengthy layover or a delayed trip.

The airport features a movie theater, a rooftop pool, and even a butterfly enclosure where visitors can get up close and personal with real butterflies.

Overall, traveling through Changi Airport to get to Singapore is a memorable experience. The airport genuinely sets the bar for airport travel across the world with its first-rate amenities, magnificent design, and selection of amenities.

Bus

Bus travel can be a practical and economical way to get to Singapore. An comprehensive network of bus routes connects Singapore to Malaysia, making it simple for tourists to travel there by bus. It is simple to go around the city-state after you arrive thanks to a number of bus stations that are conveniently positioned around the metropolis.

The first task you must complete after arriving by bus in Singapore is going through immigration. At the border, you will have to go through immigration and customs if you are traveling from Malaysia. When you arrive in Singapore, the immigration officer will require your passport and other travel documents. Singapore has stringent immigration requirements, therefore it's critical to follow them exactly to prevent any problems.

You can take your luggage and head to the bus terminal after clearing immigration. The Woodlands Regional Bus Interchange, Golden Mile Complex, and the Singapore Flyer are just a few of the bus terminals in Singapore. It is simple to get around because these terminals are well connected to the city's public transportation system, which includes the MRT and buses.

Purchasing an EZ-link card or a Singapore Tourist Pass is advised if you are a first-time visitor to Singapore in order to facilitate getting around the city. All forms of public transportation, including buses and railways, accept these cards.

In general, traveling to Singapore by bus can be simple and convenient. Getting throughout the city is simple and economical because to the well-developed public transportation system and the strategically placed bus stations. To ensure a smooth journey, don't forget to follow immigration regulations and buy an EZ-link card or Singapore Tourist Pass.

Train

Any traveler can enjoy the thrill of arriving in Singapore by rail. The opportunity to take in the magnificent grandeur of the surrounding landscape on the train ride into the city-state is unmatched. Beautiful views of Singapore's skyline, clear waterways, and lush vegetation will meet you as you get closer.

You'll be astounded by how advanced and effective the transit system is once you get to the railway station. You can easily travel throughout Singapore thanks to the MRT system, a top-notch network that connects the whole city-state. Your EZ-Link card, a contactless card that offers discounted tickets and can be used on other modes of public transportation, can be used to purchase your MRT ticket at the station.

The bustle of Singapore's bustling city life will meet you as soon as you exit the railway station. You are in for a treat because the city-state is known for its many different ethnicities, lively street markets, and delectable cuisine. The Marina Bay Sands, an imposing three-tower structure with a rooftop infinity pool and breathtaking views of the city, is one of Singapore's must-see sights.
The Gardens by the Bay, a futuristic park with imposing Supertrees and an inside waterfall, is another popular destination.

You may also explore the colorful Chinatown area, which is rich in history and provides a variety of food and shopping options, as well as the famous Merlion monument, a representation of Singapore's marine heritage.

Sea

Using marine transportation to get to Singapore offers a special experience that lets you view the city-state from a different angle. The city-state, which is in the center of Southeast Asia, is well recognized for its striking skyline, busy streets, and rich cultural diversity. If you enter Singapore by sea, you will be met with the sight of soaring skyscrapers, active ports, and a dynamic cityscape that is guaranteed to capture your attention.

The busy port area with its big container ships and freight vessels is the first thing you'll notice as you get closer to the city-state. Ships from all over the world frequently dock at Singapore's port, which is one of the busiest in the world and handles a sizable amount of international trade.

As soon as you dock, you'll be in the middle of the city. The port is next to Marina Bay, the most well-known and scenic area in Singapore. Some of the city's most recognizable monuments, including the Marina Bay Sands hotel, the Singapore Flyer, and the Gardens by the Bay, are located in this region. You can take a leisurely stroll around the bay region while taking in the city's sights, sounds, and stunning skyline.

There are numerous alternatives open to you if you'd like to explore Singapore more. The Merlion statue, the National Gallery, and the Singapore Botanic Gardens are just a few of the famous sites you may see on a tour of the city. As an alternative, you may visit one of the city-state's many malls to indulge in some retail therapy.

Getting Around

Mass Rapid Transport

The Mass Rapid Transport (MRT) system is in the vanguard of Singapore's public transportation system, which is among the most effective and extensive in the world. One of the easiest and most reasonably priced methods to travel about Singapore is to use the MRT, a train system that covers the entire island and has more than 120 stations.

An EZ-Link card, a stored-value card that let you to pay for your train fare, is required to utilize the MRT. Any MRT station or convenience store will sell you an EZ-Link card, and you can add money to the card's balance at any time. The fare can cost between S$0.80 and S$2.50 and varies on the distance traveled.

The North-South Line (NSL), East-West Line (EWL), Circle Line (CCL), Downtown Line (DTL), and Thomson-East Coast Line (TEL) are the five primary lines that make up the MRT system. You can easily find your way around because each line has a different color. You may navigate using the obvious signs and announcements in English, Chinese, Malay, and Tamil.

Trains arrive every two to three minutes during peak hours and every five to seven minutes during non-peak hours on a daily basis from 5:30 am to midnight on the MRT. You can take a taxi or a bus to get home if you miss the final train.

Singapore has an extensive bus network in addition to the MRT, which is also connected to the MRT system. Your EZ-Link card can also be used to pay for bus fare.

The buses run continuously, with night buses running from midnight until six in the morning.

Overall, using Singapore's Mass Rapid Transit system to go around is simple, practical, and reasonably priced. You won't have any trouble finding your way around the city because to its vast network, frequent trains, and informative signage and announcements.

Bus

An effective transportation infrastructure in Singapore's thriving city-state makes traveling around a breeze. Taking the bus is one of the easiest and most reasonably priced ways to get around the city. Singapore's public transportation system is user-friendly and dependable, with a vast network of more than 300 bus lines.

An EZ-Link card, which can be used to pay for bus fares as well as those for other public transportation options like the MRT (mass rapid transit) system, is required to get started. Any MRT station, bus interchange, or convenience store sells these cards. At any of these places, you can also add money to your card's balance.

Once you have your EZ-Link card, you can board any bus and pay for your fare by tapping your card on the reader at the entrance. Bus stops prominently display bus routes, but you may also plan your itinerary and locate the closest bus stop using Google Maps or other navigational apps.

The majority of buses in Singapore are air-conditioned and have plush seats, allowing for a comfortable ride. Additionally, many buses offer free WiFi so that you may stay connected while traveling.

Ask the bus driver for advice or consult the TransitLink Journey Planner website or mobile app if you're unsure which bus to take. You can select your starting place and destination in this tool, and it will give you a list of suggested bus routes, along with estimated travel times and prices.

Bicycle

Singapore is a tiny city-state with an advanced transportation network. Cycling is growing more and more common among locals and visitors alike, even if public transportation provides an effective method to get around. Singapore is a terrific area to explore on two wheels because to its level topography, well-maintained roads, and wide network of bicycle lanes. Here are some pointers about using a bicycle to navigate Singapore.

First and foremost, those who want to pedal around the city frequently choose to hire bicycles. Numerous bike rental businesses provide a range of bicycles, including city bikes, road bikes, and mountain bikes. Depending on the kind of bike and length of the rental, the cost of renting a bike can range from S$6 to S$12 per hour. Ofo, Mobike, and SG Bike are three well-known providers of bicycle rentals.

The large system of bicycle trails that crisscross the city is one of the nicest aspects of cycling in Singapore. In Singapore, there are more than 400 kilometers of bike pathways that link the city's parks, districts, and main attractions. These routes are safe for cyclists of all abilities since they are clearly designated and kept apart from motor traffic.

Singapore's attractions can be enjoyedly explored by bicycle as well. The Marina Bay Sands loop, which provides breathtaking views of the city skyline, and the East shore Park route, which follows the shore and has a variety of food and beverage options, are two of the more well-known cycling routes. The Bukit Timah path and the Pulau Ubin trail are two more well-liked cycling routes that present more difficult terrain to seasoned bikers.

Boat

Being an island city-state, Singapore makes use of water transportation as a practical and distinctive mode of transportation. The city's attractions and sites are simple to tour by boat thanks to the many options available.

Taking a river cruise is one of the most well-liked water transportation options in Singapore. The Marina Bay Sands, the Merlion statue, and the Esplanade can all be seen from the Singapore River, which cuts through the center of the city. There are various jetties along the river where people can get on and off boats at their convenience. The river excursions can be taken during the day or at night, and many offer a commentary on the history and culture of the city.

The bumboat is another well-liked type of watercraft. Traditional boats known as bumboats were historically used to convey cargo along the Singapore River. They now provide a distinctive method for tourists to discover the city's waterways. Bumboats normally depart from Clarke Quay and transport tourists on beautiful tours of the Singapore River while passing by old shophouses and under bridges. Bumboats also provide a distinctive viewpoint of the city's contemporary buildings, including the soaring Marina Bay Sands and the ArtScience Museum.

Visitors can take ferries to surrounding islands like Sentosa and Pulau Ubin in addition to river cruises and bumboats. Numerous attractions, including theme parks, beaches, and nature walks, can be found on these islands. Ferries provide a simple method to get out from the city and discover Singapore's natural beauty; they mainly leave from Marina South Pier or HarbourFront Centre.

Car or Motorcycle

With its sophisticated infrastructure and effective transportation networks, getting around Singapore is simple with a vehicle or motorcycle. Prior to selecting a means of transportation, it is crucial to carefully consider the advantages and disadvantages of each possibilities.

In order to discourage car ownership and ease traffic congestion, the government of Singapore levies hefty taxes and fees on vehicles, making driving a car expensive. However, a car can be a practical and pleasant alternative for those who need to travel across great distances or transport large objects. Driving is safe and simple in Singapore because to its well-developed road network, adequate signage, and other safety elements. Drivers should be prepared for some delays, though, as traffic can be congested during peak hours, particularly in the central business district. Due to limited space and exorbitant parking rates in some places, parking might be difficult as well.

On the other hand, riding a motorcycle in Singapore can be an affordable and practical choice, particularly for quick excursions within the city. Motorcycles are a cheap option for many because they are excluded from the heavy taxes and fees placed on cars. The well-maintained network of highways and expressways in Singapore makes motorcycling quick and effective. Safety is a worry, though, as motorcyclists are more likely to be involved in collisions than cars. Riders need to be especially cautious on the roads and carry the proper safety gear. Additionally, parking a motorcycle is typically less expensive and simpler than parking a car.

Overall, there are benefits and drawbacks to using motorcycles and vehicles to navigate around Singapore. Before choosing a means of transportation, it's vital to take into account elements including cost, convenience, safety, and trip requirements. Driving might be the best choice for people who can afford the high expenditures of automobile ownership and want the comfort of a car. A motorcycle can be the best alternative for people looking for a more practical and cheap means of transportation for short distances. In the end, the decision is based on personal tastes and circumstances.

Chapter 3

Top Attractions in Singapore

SENTOSA ISLAND

Sights

Top Experience: get your thrills at Universal Studio

Singapore's Sentosa Island is a well-liked vacation spot with a variety of fun activities and attractions. Sentosa Island offers something for everyone, from breathtaking beaches and world-class entertainment parks to historical monuments and cultural events. Some of the prominent attractions on Sentosa Island are listed below:

More than 20 thrilling rides and attractions based on well-known motion pictures and television shows can be found at the renowned theme park in Singapore known as Universal Studios. Universal Studios

Singapore is a must-see attraction for people of all ages, including thrilling rides like Transformers: The Ride 3D and family-friendly attractions like the Sesame Street Spaghetti Space Chase.

Siloso Beach is one of the three main beaches on Sentosa Island and a well-liked location for swimming, water sports, and tanning. Kayaks, paddleboards, and other watercraft can be rented by visitors. Alternatively, they can choose to unwind on the beach with a drink from one of the surrounding bars or restaurants.

S.E.A. Aquarium: This enormous aquarium is one of the biggest in the world, housing more than 100,000 marine animals from more than 1,000 species. In the aquarium's several exhibits, visitors can see vibrant fish, beautiful sharks, and other underwater species.

Fort Siloso is a well-preserved military structure from the late 19th century that gives visitors a look at Singapore's past. The fort features an underground network of tunnels that can be visited and a museum with artifacts about the island's military past.

One of Sentosa Island's most distinctive features is the 37-meter-tall Sentosa Merlion, a statue of a half-lion, half-fish creature. For breathtaking views of the island and the surrounding sea, visitors can climb to the top of the statue.

Sentosa Island, in addition to these prominent attractions, also features the Adventure Cove Waterpark, the Butterfly Park and Insect Kingdom, as well as the Sentosa Island Beaches. Sentosa Island is guaranteed to have something to suit your tastes, whether you're seeking for excitement, relaxation, or cultural immersion.

Eating

Tourists that travel to Singapore frequently visit Sentosa Island. Beaches, theme parks, and resorts are just a few of the island's many attractions. Sentosa Island has a wide variety of dining options, making dining there a pleasant experience.

The Quayside Isle is one of Sentosa Island's top dining establishments. Numerous eateries in this neighborhood offer stunning marina views. Italian, Japanese, and Mediterranean food are just a few of the options offered by the eateries. The Sole Pomodoro Trattoria Pizzeria is one of Quayside Isle's most well-liked eateries. It offers genuine Italian cuisine, including wood-fired pizza and fresh pasta.

Resorts World Sentosa is another dining option on Sentosa Island. There are several different dining options available at this resort, including Western, Chinese, and

Malaysian food. The Malaysian Food Street is one of this resort's most well-liked eateries. It provides a variety of Malaysian cuisine, including Laksa and Nasi Lemak.

The Sentosa Cove is a fantastic restaurant for seafood lovers. There are numerous seafood establishments in this region that provide freshly caught seafood. The Fisherman's Wharf is one of Sentosa Cove's well-known seafood establishments. A variety of seafood is available, including lobster, oysters, and crabs.

The Ocean Restaurant by Cat Cora is a must-visit if you're seeking for a distinctive dining experience. An expansive view of the marine life can be seen from this café, which is inside the S.E.A. Aquarium. It offers Mediterranean fare like lamb rack and grilled octopus.

Drinking & Nightlife

One of Singapore's liveliest and most well-liked tourist sites is Sentosa Island. It provides guests with a wide variety of alternatives for drinking and nightlife, from upscale rooftop bars to active beach clubs.

Tanjong Beach Club, which is situated on Tanjong Beach, is one of the busiest bars on Sentosa Island. The beach club has a relaxed ambiance and inviting daybeds and cabanas. It offers a vast range of wines and a variety of cocktails, making it ideal for a relaxing afternoon with friends.

Another well-liked location is the Skyline Luge Sentosa, which provides breathtaking views of the city skyline while sipping a cool beverage. It's the perfect place to escape the city's noise and chaos and enjoy the peace and beauty of the island.

The Hard Rock Cafe Sentosa is a must-see for visitors looking for a lively atmosphere. It offers live music, wonderful food, and a variety of drinks, and is close to the Universal Studios Singapore. The location is well-liked by both visitors and residents and is ideal for a night out with friends.

Visit the 1-Altitude at The Outpost Hotel if you're seeking for a bar with a view. On the 64th level, this rooftop bar provides stunning views of the downtown cityscape. The bar serves a variety of beers and cocktails and is a great place to watch the sunset with your loved ones.

Finally, beach clubs like Ola Beach Club or FOC Sentosa are the best places to go if you want to party all night. These clubs are the ideal spot to dance the night away because they provide a wide selection of drinks and live DJs.

Entertainment

One of the most well-liked tourist sites in Singapore is Sentosa Island, which provides guests with a variety of entertainment alternatives. The island is well-known for its beautiful beaches, thrilling attractions, and top-notch entertainment venues, which make it the ideal vacation spot for groups of friends, families, and lovers.

Universal Studios Singapore is one of Sentosa Island's most well-liked entertainment destinations. This theme park offers exhilarating rides, live performances, and attractions based on well-known films and television series. Visitors can immerse themselves in the fantasy of the movies and meet their favorite movie characters, such as Shrek, Jurassic Park, and the Transformers.

The Adventure Cove Waterpark is the ideal location for individuals who prefer water-based activities. For hours of pleasure, visitors of all ages can enjoy the variety of water slides, lazy rivers, and wave pools at this waterpark. The Rainbow Reef also offers snorkeling opportunities for visitors to have up close encounters with aquatic life.

From informal cafes to luxury dining establishments, Sentosa Island offers a variety of dining alternatives. Visitors can sample a wide range of cuisines, including international, seafood, and Singaporean fare. On Sentosa Island, among of the well-liked restaurants are Tanjong Beach Club, The Cliff, and Ocean Restaurant by Cat Cora.

Sentosa Island has a variety of pubs and nightclubs that are ideal for a night out if you appreciate the nightlife. Tanjong Beach Club, a renowned beach club with live music, cocktails, and a breathtaking sunset view, is located on the island.

Sentosa Island has a variety of entertainment activities that are catered to all tastes and interests. Sentosa Island offers a variety of entertainment options for all visitors, whether they're searching for a romantic evening out or family-friendly fun.

Sports & Activities

A variety of sports and activities are available for guests to enjoy on Sentosa Island, a stunning resort island off the coast of Singapore. Sentosa Island features activities for everyone, whether they are looking for excitement or relaxation.

Golf is one of the most well-liked sports on Sentosa Island. The Serapong and the Tanjong are two championship golf courses located on the island. Both courses are built to test golfers of all skill levels and offer breathtaking views of the island and the South China Sea.

Sentosa Island has a variety of water activities available for those that want them. Visitors can try their hand at surfing, stand-up paddleboarding, and kayaking. The Wave House, which offers a simulated surfing experience ideal for both novice and expert surfers, is another attraction on the island.

Sentosa Island offers a variety of thrilling activities if an adrenaline rush is what you're after. The MegaZip, Southeast Asia's largest zip line, is located on the island, as is the Skyline Luge, an exhilarating ride that transports passengers in a tiny cart down a curving track.

Sentosa Island offers a variety of wellness and spa alternatives for those looking for a more tranquil experience. Visitors can indulge in a range of services like massages, facials, and body wraps in addition to taking yoga and meditation lessons.

Sentosa Island offers a wide variety of attractions in addition to sports and activities. The island's beaches can be explored, a nature walk can be taken, and the famous Merlion monument can be seen. A number of top-notch eateries, shopping malls, and entertainment venues can be found on the island.

In general, sports and activity aficionados will find Sentosa Island to be a dream. There are plenty of activities to do on this lovely island, including golf, water sports, and heart-pounding adventures.

THE BOTANIC GARDENS

Top Experience: Stroll in Singapore Botanic Gardens

Sights

A large and impressive public park called The Botanic Gardens can be found in the center of numerous cities all over the world. The gardens offer a wide variety of plant life from all over the world in addition to a number of other attractions, making it a must-visit location for both visitors and locals. Here are some examples of sights you could encounter when visiting a botanical garden.

The magnificent plant life at the Botanic Gardens is what makes them famous in the first place. A vast range of plants, including trees, shrubs, flowers, and other flora, can be found in the gardens. Visitors can anticipate seeing a variety of international species, from tropical flora to desert cacti. The gardens are often laid out such that each plant is shown off in the best possible way, with well-kept trails meandering among the many exhibits.

The Botanic Gardens offer a number of other attractions in addition to the flora. For instance, many gardens incorporate water features, such as ponds, lakes, and fountains, which enhance the park's natural attractiveness. Many different types of wildlife, such as ducks, swans, and other waterfowl, are drawn to these water features.

The numerous sculptures and other pieces of art that are dotted all across Botanic Gardens are another well-liked attraction. These works of art can be appreciated both as works of art and as a component of the overall park experience. They frequently enhance the natural beauty of the plants and other garden features.

The gardens are a well-liked location for performances and activities. There are outdoor amphitheaters and other performance venues in many parks where concerts, plays, and other events are held. These activities can enhance the park's already remarkable atmosphere and offer a unique way to see the Botanic Gardens.

Many botanic gardens offer educational programs and tours for anyone who are interested in learning more about the plants and other aspects of the garden. From young children to adults, these programs may be modified to fit their needs and interests, and they can be a terrific way to increase your understanding of nature.

The Botanic Gardens are also a great spot to decompress and unwind, to sum it up. They provide a nice escape from the bustle of daily life with their calm mood, well-kept lawns, and beautiful environment. The Botanic Gardens are a nice location to relax and read a book, have a picnic, or just take in the view.

Sidebar is open

Eating

Botanical gardens are lovely, serene places with a wealth of plant life. Many tourists spend hours wandering the gardens, appreciating the flora, and soaking in the landscape since they provide a wonderful opportunity to get in touch with nature. It is understandable why picnickers and alfresco diners enjoy visiting botanic gardens. Here are some reasons why dining in a botanical garden can be a genuinely unique experience:

It all starts with the idyllic location. The lush vegetation, vibrant flowers, and tranquil water features provide a tranquil atmosphere ideal for relaxing and unwinding. The botanic garden offers a beautiful backdrop that enhances the dining experience, whether you're having a family get-together or a romantic picnic with your significant other.

Additionally, botanic gardens provide a variety of dining alternatives, including cafes, restaurants, and packed lunches. You can bring your own food and choose a peaceful place to eat it, or you can go to one of the garden's cafes or restaurants. Numerous botanic gardens provide fresh, wholesome produce that is locally produced and in season.

Eating at botanical gardens also offers the chance to discover more about the plants and their use. The origin, cultural value, and therapeutic properties of the plants are all described in detail on the informational signs that are common in botanic gardens. Thus, dining in a botanical garden might be a fantastic opportunity to learn more about plants.

Last but not least, dining in botanic gardens is a sustainable and green option. Compostable packaging is used at many botanic gardens, and they encourage visitors to bring their own containers in order to reduce waste and promote sustainability. You may help the neighborhood and the environment by opting to eat at a restaurant located in a botanical garden.

Shopping & Activities

The Botanic Gardens are a stunning and sizable park that can be found in many cities all over the world. They provide a serene refuge amidst the rush of urban life. The gardens are frequently a well-liked destination for both locals and visitors to unwind, wander, and take in the wonders of nature. But the Botanic Gardens provide much more than just a serene setting. They provide tourists with a wealth of entertainment and engaging activities, as well as a fantastic setting for shopping.

It can be interesting to shop at the Botanic Gardens. Many of the gardens have gift stores where visitors can purchase souvenirs and garden-related goods. These stores frequently stock local crafts and artwork as well as books on botany, gardening equipment, and gardening supplies. Plant seeds, gardening manuals, and other products linked to gardens may also be available in the shops.

Many of the Botanic Gardens also hold farmers' markets and other events where guests can purchase for locally produced foods, artisanal goods, and handmade crafts in addition to the gift shops. These markets offer a special chance for tourists to interact with local growers and artisans, and they are frequently hosted on weekends or other set days.

The Botanic Gardens have a wide variety of activities available. Simply taking a leisurely stroll through the gardens is a common pastime. Numerous gardens have well-kept walks that weave through the various plant collections and provide breathtaking views of the surroundings. Take your time, take in the sunshine and fresh air, and take in the beauty of the gardens at your own speed.

The Botanic Gardens provide a variety of additional activities for individuals who prefer to be more active. Visitors can have a leisurely lunch or snack while surrounded by the natural splendor of the gardens at several of the grounds' designated picnic sites. Some gardens also have kid-friendly playgrounds, giving youngsters a fun and secure place to play while their parents tour the grounds.

Bird viewing is another well-liked activity at the Botanic Gardens. A large range of bird species call many of the gardens home, and visitors frequently see them darting around amid the trees and flowers. To give guests the chance to learn more about the local bird population and their role in the garden environment, some gardens even provide guided bird watching tours.

Many botanic gardens provide educational programs and guided tours for people who want to learn more about the gardens and the plants that grow there. These programs might discuss a range of subjects, including plant identification, gardening methods, and conservation initiatives. Visitors can learn from skilled professionals and develop a deeper understanding of the significance and beauty of the gardens.

SOUTHWEST & WEST SINGAPORE

Sights

The tiny city-state of Singapore, located in Southeast Asia, is frequently referred to as a city-state. Singapore, despite its tiny size, is crammed with sights to see, especially in the southwest and west parts of the island. There is something for everyone to enjoy in these regions, from breathtaking parks and museums to charming neighborhoods and cultural relics. The main attractions in Southwest and West Singapore are listed below.

The Gardens by the Bay is one of Singapore's most well-liked tourist destinations. The Gardens by the Bay, a horticultural wonderland covering more than 100 hectares, is home to gorgeous outdoor gardens, a sizable greenhouse complex, and a number of attractions like the Supertree Grove and the Cloud Forest Dome. The Cloud Forest Dome has a 35-meter indoor waterfall, a foggy cloud forest, and unusual plant life from tropical highlands, while the Supertree Grove is a collection of towering tree-like structures covered with more than 200 different kinds of plants and flowers. The Flower Dome, Heritage Gardens, and Bay East Garden, which provides sweeping views of the Marina Bay skyline, are some of the additional features of Gardens by the Bay.

Sentosa Island is yet another must-see destination in Southwest Singapore. This well-known vacation island can be reached by cable car, monorail, or bridge and offers a variety of activities and attractions. Visitors can take leisurely strolls along the island's beautiful beaches, indulge in some retail therapy at Resorts World Sentosa, or visit the S.E.A. Aquarium to witness more than 100,000 aquatic animals representing 1,000 different species. Other points of interest on Sentosa Island include the entertainment park Universal Studios Singapore, the Skyline Luge Sentosa, and the enormous monument of Singapore's national emblem, the Sentosa Merlion.

Moving on to Singapore's West, one of the most well-known sites is the Haw Par Villa. With more than 1,000 statues and dioramas depicting scenarios from Chinese folklore, such as the Ten Courts of Hell, the Journey to the West, and the Romance of the Three Kingdoms, this one-of-a-kind theme park is centered on Chinese mythology. Haw Boon and Par Boon, the brothers of the park's creators who also founded the Tiger Balm business, are honored in the park's name.

Visitors can take part in cultural performances, guided tours, and traditional Chinese ceremonies in addition to exploring the park's different displays.

Jurong Bird Park is yet another well-liked tourist destination in West Singapore. Home to approximately 5,000 birds from 400 species, the park is a treat for bird lovers and ornithologists. It is possible for visitors to take a leisurely stroll through the park's numerous aviaries and exhibitions, enjoy live bird shows, and even interact closely with some of the birds at feeding times and other opportunities. The African Waterfall Aviary, the Penguin Coast, and the Lory Loft, where visitors can feed the vibrant lorikeets, are some of the highlights of the Jurong Bird Park.

Tiong Bahru is one of West Singapore's most scenic neighborhoods. This quaint residential neighborhood is renowned for its distinctive Art Deco architecture, cool cafes, and cutting-edge stores. Visitors can stroll around the neighborhood's narrow lanes and alleyways, taking in the vibrant shophouses and unique shops while savoring regional specialties like kaya toast and traditional kopi. Tiong Bahru is a well-liked vacation spot for artists and designers due to the abundance of art galleries, bookstores, and design studios there.

Eating

The southwest and west of the city-state are no exception to Singapore's reputation for its dynamic and diversified cuisine culture. There are numerous restaurants in these places that serve a variety of flavors and cuisines to suit every preference and price range.

The southwest and west regions of Singapore share this tradition of hawker centers with the rest of the country. The

Jurong West Hawker Centre is a must-visit if you're searching for a quick, inexpensive, and delectable dinner. Many hawker booths offering local specialties including chicken rice, char kway teow, and laksa can be found here. Another well-liked alternative is the Bukit Timah Market and Food Centre, which offers a selection of traditional Singaporean dishes like satay, prawn noodles, and Hokkien mee.

For those who want to indulge in seafood, there are several restaurants in the West Coast Seafood Centre that serve a variety of seafood delicacies, such as butter prawns, chili crab, and black pepper crab. Visit the Keppel Bay harbor for a more premium eating experience. There, you can choose from a number of waterfront eateries that serve up delectable foreign fare while providing gorgeous harbor views.

Visit Pasir Panjang Road, which is renowned for its broad variety of international food, if you want to experience something new. Everything from Mexican tacos to Japanese ramen to Korean BBQ can be found here. The region is a great choice for health-conscious eaters as it also has a number of vegan and vegetarian restaurants.

Overall, Singapore's southwest and west regions provide a wide variety of dining options to suit every taste and budget. Everyone can find something to eat, whether they like fancy waterfront dining or inexpensive hawker fare. Therefore, whether you're a local or a visitor, make sure to learn about the local food scene and sample some of the city-state's best dishes.

Drinking & Nightlife

Singapore's southwest and west feature a thriving nightlife culture with a wide range of drinking establishments for both locals and tourists. Here are a few of the well-liked destinations for a night out:

For young residents and foreigners looking for a fun night out, Holland Village is a popular choice. There are numerous taverns, pubs, and clubs in the region that may accommodate a variety of interests and preferences. Wala Wala Cafe Bar, Harry's Bar, and Lorong Mambong are a few of the hotspots.

Clarke Quay: Clarke Quay is a well-known nightlife area in Singapore. Clarke Quay, which is situated along the Singapore River, is a bustling area with a wide selection of pubs, clubs, and eateries. The hot spots to visit are Zouk, Attica, and Crazy Elephant.

Sentosa Island: Sentosa Island in Singapore is a well-liked vacation spot and has a number of bars and nightclubs. Visitors can dance the night away at Azzura

Beach Club or take part in a beach party at Tanjong Beach Club.

Choa Chu Kang: Choa Chu Kang boasts a number of well-liked drinking establishments for those seeking a more local experience. There are many hawker centers in the neighborhood where tourists may eat and drink regional fare. For a night out, people frequently visit Junction 10 and Lot One Shoppers' Mall.

Jurong East: Another place with a developing nightlife scene is Jurong East. Numerous bars and clubs can be found in the vicinity, including The Beast and BAROSSA Bar & Bistro.

Overall, individuals wishing to enjoy a night out have many options in Southwest and West Singapore. Visitors can select from hip pubs and clubs to neighborhood hawker centers, and they can take advantage of the active nightlife culture in these places.

Entertainment

Both locals and visitors can find a variety of entertainment alternatives in Southwest and West Singapore. There are several attractions in the area, including theme parks, casinos, museums, and cultural institutions that cater to a range of interests and tastes.

The Universal Studios theme park is one of the most well-liked entertainment places in the Southwest and West of Singapore. This well-known theme park, which is situated on Sentosa Island, offers a variety of rides and attractions based on well-liked motion pictures and television shows. Roller coasters, movie sets, and live performances are all available to visitors.

The Singapore Chinese Cultural Centre is a must-visit location for anyone seeking a more cultural encounter. Through a variety of displays and events, such as musical performances, art exhibitions, and workshops, the center promotes Chinese culture and heritage.

The Resorts World Sentosa, which has a casino, an aquarium, and a number of other entertainment facilities, is another well-liked destination in the area. At the S.E.A. Aquarium, visitors can explore the underwater world. They can also ride the cable car or spend the evening gambling.

Several parks and nature reserves can be found in the West Singapore area, providing a tranquil and beautiful respite from the city. Bird enthusiasts frequently visit the Jurong Bird Park, while the Singapore Botanic Gardens, a UNESCO World Heritage Site, is known for its wide variety of plant species.

Southwest and West Singapore also have a lively nightlife culture with lots of pubs, clubs, and music venues in addition to these attractions. With its vibrant ambiance and array of entertainment options, the Clarke Quay area is a favorite party destination.

Overall, the entertainment options in Southwest and West Singapore are diversified and cater to a range of tastes and interests. There is something in this dynamic region for everyone, whether you enjoy theme parks, cultural adventures, or outdoor pursuits.

Sports & Activities

For both locals and tourists, Southwest and West Singapore provide a wide variety of sports and activities. Everyone will find something to enjoy in this region of Singapore, which offers activities including water sports, trekking, and classic sports like football and basketball.

Water sports are among the most well-liked pastimes in Southwest and West Singapore.

Numerous beaches in the region, including Sentosa and West Coast Park, offer opportunities for surfing, kayaking, and paddleboarding. There are several picturesque locations along the shore where people can go fishing or enjoy a leisurely boat ride if they want a more laid-back experience.

There are also several possibilities available for people who choose land-based activities. Numerous nature parks and reserves, including Bukit Batok Nature Park, Kent Ridge Park, and the Southern Ridges, offer a tranquil setting for hikers to explore. Hiking is a well-liked activity in the area. In addition, there are a number of outdoor sporting facilities and parks where guests can participate in pursuits like cycling, tennis, basketball, and football.

Southwest and West Singapore offer a variety of extreme sports activities for thrill-seekers, including bungee jumping, ziplining, and indoor skydiving at Sentosa Island. Additionally, visitors can practice their archery abilities at the Archery Club Singapore or go indoor rock climbing at Boulder World.

Southwest and West Singapore have several options to watch live games or take part in sports leagues for individuals who are interested in traditional sports. Local football games are played at Jurong East Stadium, and basketball fans can use the cutting-edge Singapore Basketball Centre at Kallang. Additionally, the region is home to a number of golf courses, including the Sentosa Golf Club, which serves as the venue for major international competitions like the HSBC Women's World Championship.

CHINATOWN

Sights

Chinatown is a district with a large concentration of Chinese residents and businesses in many cities all over the world. As a result, Chinatown offers a variety of attractions that showcase Chinese culture, history, and cuisine. We'll look at some of Chinatown's best attractions in this article.

Chinese Gate: The elaborate and vibrant Chinese gate that welcomes visitors to the neighborhood is one of Chinatown's most recognizable characteristics. The gate makes for a fantastic photo opportunity because it is frequently adorned with ornate dragon motifs and Chinese lettering.

Chinese Historical Society Museum: This museum chronicles the experiences and contributions of Chinese immigrants to American society throughout history. It has displays on Chinese culture, music, language, and art.

Golden Gate Fortune Cookie Factory is a well-liked tourist and local attraction because it allows visitors to see fortune cookies being made by hand and even try some of the freshly baked cookies. The factory has been running for more than 50 years and is a cherished landmark in the area.

Chinese traditional goods and souvenirs, such as teas, herbs, silk clothing, and handicrafts, are available at the markets in Chinatown. Visitors can bargain with sellers and peruse the vibrant stalls.

Chinese Temples: There are a number of accessible Chinese temples in Chinatown. Chinese deity sculptures, elaborate altars, and incense burners are common features of these temples. Visitors are welcome to observe traditional ceremonies and learn about Chinese religious customs.

Chinese food: A trip to Chinatown wouldn't be complete without trying some of the delectable local fare. There are numerous restaurants and food stalls offering everything from dim sum to noodle dishes to roasted duck. Visitors can also try bubble tea, a popular Taiwanese beverage made with tea, milk, and tapioca pearls.

Eating

Chinatown is a thriving, culturally diverse neighborhood that serves a wide range of real Chinese food. Eating in Chinatown is more than simply a way to sate your stomach—it's an immersion into a whole new world of tastes and textures that may titillate your senses.

Dim sum is one of the most well-liked foods in Chinatown. The term "dim sum" describes a range of little foods that are typically served on small plates or in bamboo baskets. These foods include pan-fried treats like turnip cakes and scallion pancakes as well as steamed buns and dumplings. Dim sum is commonly served with tea and eaten during brunch or lunch. A significant aspect of dim sum culture is the sharing and tasting of many dishes together.

Peking duck is another dish that is popular in Chinatown. With thin pancakes, scallions, and sweet bean sauce, Peking duck is a roasted duck that has been spiced with a number of different ingredients. The flesh from the duck is usually wrapped in the pancake with the other components after it has been cut at the table. A delightful and savory bite is created by the blending of flavors and textures.

Chinatown offers a wide range of additional options in addition to these traditional cuisines, including sour Sichuan food and fresh fish. Egg tarts and pineapple buns are just a couple of the sweet and savory delicacies that Chinese bakers sell.

In addition to the food itself, Chinatown's environment enhances the overall dining experience. You can travel to another time and place by strolling through the busy streets and taking in the brilliant colors and aromas of the various restaurants. It's a one-of-a-kind experience that is incomparable.

In general, dining in Chinatown offers a chance to learn about and appreciate Chinese culture through its food. Chinatown caters to all tastes, whether you're a foodie or just searching for a special dining experience.

Drinking & Nightlife

Known for its rich history and customs, which are reflected in its thriving nightlife scene, Chinatown is a thriving neighborhood. Chinatown, a well-liked tourist destination, has a variety of drinking and nightlife alternatives to suit a variety of interests and inclinations.

The rooftop bar at the Hotel 50 Bowery is one of the most popular places to drink in Chinatown. This chic bar provides a selection of artisan cocktails and small appetizers while providing magnificent views of the metropolitan skyline. The rooftop bar is the ideal location for a date or a fun night out with friends.

Apotheke is a speakeasy-style bar that provides a unique drinking experience for those seeking a more relaxed ambiance. An comprehensive selection of handcrafted drinks, many of which are inspired by traditional Chinese medicines and ingredients, is offered at this cozy bar, which is nestled away in a back alley.

One of the city's oldest dim sum establishments, Nom Wah Tea Parlor, offers visitors a sense of Chinatown's long heritage. This famous location attracts both locals and tourists due to its distinctive combination of traditional Chinese tea and dim lunch.

In addition, there are many karaoke bars in Chinatown where guests can sing along with friends in a cozy setting. A well-liked destination for karaoke fans is K-One Karaoke, which provides individual rooms with cutting-edge sound systems and a huge collection of songs in several languages.

The drinking and nightlife culture in Chinatown generally has something to offer everyone. The nightlife options in Chinatown reflect the neighborhood's unique history and customs, whether visitors are seeking for a hip rooftop bar or a quaint speakeasy.

Shopping

A thriving cultural area known as Chinatown may be found in many large cities all over the world. Chinatown is a terrific destination to buy for a wide range of goods and services because of its distinctive architecture, lively ambiance, and bustling street markets.

The broad selection of economical and distinctive goods that are offered is one of Chinatown's key draws for shoppers. Visitors can get everything they need, from traditional Chinese herbal cures and teas to unusual cuisines, jewelry, apparel, and handicrafts. Additionally, a lot of the shops and stalls offer deals and discounts, making it a great place for consumers on a tight budget.

Shopping in Chinatown offers the chance to learn about another culture, which is one of its best features. Visitors will undoubtedly be transported to another universe by the sights, sounds, and fragrances of the neighborhood. They can browse the many traditional Chinese shops and markets, eat some real Chinese food, and discover more about the culture's traditions and history.

The street markets are among the most well-liked locations in Chinatown for shopping. These vibrant and active markets are teeming with stalls offering a wide variety of goods, including apparel, souvenirs, antiques, fresh produce, and seafood. The marketplaces are ideal places to practice haggling and negotiating, and customers can frequently receive a better deal by doing so.

A large variety of dining establishments serving Chinese and Asian food may be found in Chinatown. Visitors can enjoy in a great and authentic meal while taking a break from shopping, from dim sum and noodles to hot pot and BBQ.

In conclusion, shopping in Chinatown is a distinctive and fun experience that shouldn't be missed. Visitors are sure to find what they're searching for in this lively and colorful sector, whether they're looking for a distinctive souvenir, an original gift, or just a taste of another culture.

Activities

A cultural center, Chinatown provides a wide range of activities for both locals and visitors. Located in major cities around the world, Chinatown is known for its vibrant atmosphere, delicious food, and unique shopping experiences. Here are some of the activities that you may enjoy in Chinatown:

Discover the sights and architecture. Chinatown is renowned for its unusual architecture, which combines modern and traditional Chinese designs. Take a stroll around the neighborhood and admire the ornate buildings, colorful temples, and beautiful gardens. Even famous landmarks like the Chinatown Gate, a representation of the cultural importance of Chinatown, may be found in various cities.

Try the food - Chinatown is a food lover's paradise. There are many real Chinese meals available, including dim sum, dumplings, noodles, and shellfish. Chinese pastries, teas, and herbal remedies can also be found in specialty stores. Don't forget to try bubble tea, a popular drink that originated in Taiwan and has become a staple in Chinatown cafes.

Shop for souvenirs - Chinatown is home to many unique shops that sell souvenirs, clothing, and trinkets. You can find traditional Chinese clothing, handcrafted jewelry, and even rare books and antiques. Numerous stores also offer traditional Chinese goods like kites, lanterns, and calligraphy brushes.

Attend cultural activities; as a center of culture, Chinatown frequently hosts festivals and other celebrations of Chinese culture. These events include Chinese New Year, Dragon Boat Festival, and Mid-Autumn Festival. During these festivals, you may anticipate seeing vibrant parades, lion dances, and fireworks.

Visit museums and galleries - Chinatown is also home to many museums and galleries that showcase Chinese art and culture. These include the Museum of Chinese in America in New York, the Chinese American Museum in Los Angeles, and the Wing Luke Museum of the Asian Pacific American Experience in Seattle.

LITTLE INDIA

Sights

In the center of Singapore, there is a bustling and colorful district called Little

India. Visitors can learn about the rich histories and traditions of the Indian community in this hive of activity and melting pot of cultures. The following are a few of the top Little India attractions:

Sri Veeramakaliamman Temple Is one of Little India's most well-known sights. The temple, which honors the Hindu goddess Kali, is renowned for its elaborate carvings and vibrant ornamentation. Visitors can observe the daily devotional rites and offerings to the deity and learn about Hinduism.

Mustafa Centre is a sizable shopping center that is open every day of the year. It serves as a one-stop shop for everything from groceries and spices to gadgets and clothing. For travelers who wish to experience the commotion of Little India, it is a must-visit location.

Tekka Centre is lively market offers a glimpse into Little India's sights, sounds, and aromas. It is a fantastic location to buy souvenirs, fresh fruit, and traditional Indian apparel. Additionally, tourists can enjoy regional specialties including roti prata, biryani, and teh tarik.

Little India Arcade is a vibrant boulevard lined with stores offering ethnic Indian apparel, jewelry, and handicrafts. Shop-hopping visitors might find one-of-a-kind trinkets to bring back home.

The museum known as the Indian Heritage Centre highlights the history, culture, and contributions of the Indian population in Singapore. It is a fantastic location to discover the origins of the Indian people and their migration to Singapore.

The House of Tan Teng Niah is an elegant, vividly colored structure that is a favorite Instagram location. It was constructed in the early 1900s by a Chinese businessman for his Indian wife and is today seen as a representation of Singapore's multiculturalism.

Eating

A pleasant experience that immerses guests in the vivacious and colorful culture of Indian cuisine is dining in Little India. Little India, a thriving district in the center of Singapore, is well-known for its energetic streets, vibrant shops, and delicious cuisine. There is a wide variety of Indian restaurants in this area, serving everything from high-end gourmet dining to traditional street food.

The biryani, a fragrant and tasty rice dish cooked with aromatic spices, veggies, and meats, is one of the must-try foods in Little India. The biryani is frequently served with papadum, a crunchy flatbread made of lentils, and raita, a cool yogurt-based dip.

Butter chicken, tandoori chicken, and fish head curry are among more well-known Indian specialties in Little India.

Along with its savory cuisine, Little India is renowned for its desserts and sweets. Rasgulla, a sweet and juicy cheese ball drenched in syrup, and gulab jamun, a soft and spongy milk-based confection, are two of the most well-liked sweets. The kulfi, a thick and creamy Indian ice cream prepared with condensed milk and flavored with cardamom, saffron, and pistachios, is another treat you must try.

Little India, in addition to its delectable cuisine, also provides a distinctive cultural experience with its vibrant temples, complex architecture, and energetic festivals. The Sakya Muni Buddha Gaya Temple is a tranquil Buddhist temple with a sizable golden Buddha statue, while the Sri Veeramakaliamman Temple is a magnificent Hindu temple devoted to the goddess Kali.

Drinking & Nightlife

Singapore's Little India is a thriving district distinguished by its vibrant streets, flavorful cuisine, and ethnic festivals. It's also a fantastic location for people seeking a fun night on the town. Little India has a lot to offer, whether you want to go out for a few drinks with friends or check out the local nightlife.

The Tekka Centre is one of Little India's most well-liked bars. Numerous hawker booths providing regional specialties including satay, nasi lemak, and biryani can be found here. Drink a cool beer or beverage from one of the many pubs nearby to wash it all down. Weekends are when the Tekka Centre is busiest, and both locals and visitors may be found taking advantage of the bustling environment.

There are many options available for those seeking to enjoy Little India's nightlife. The Blu Jaz Cafe, which has live music, DJs, and a dance floor, is one of the most well-liked locations. With a blend of locals and visitors, the ambiance is vibrant and eclectic.

The Mustafa Centre, a nightlife hotspot open round-the-clock in Little India, is another well-known location. The center's karaoke room is located on the top floor and is a terrific spot to let free and sing your heart out with friends. The facility also includes a rooftop bar where you can unwind with a drink and see the breathtaking cityscape.

In conclusion, Little India is a fantastic location for anyone seeking a fun night out in Singapore. It's simple to understand why this neighborhood is a favorite among residents and visitors alike with its vibrant environment, delectable cuisine, and varied selection of pubs and nightlife locations.

Shopping

The busy ethnic district of Little India is situated in the center of Singapore. The thriving area is a fusion of Indian cuisine, culture, and retail. With a vast variety of stores and markets selling anything from exotic spices and jewelry to traditional Indian apparel, Little India offers a shopping experience unlike any other. A thorough guide to shopping in Little India may be found here.

The Mustafa Centre is one of Little India's most well-liked shopping areas. This 24-hour shopping center is renowned for its wide range of products, which includes electronics, apparel, jewelry, and trinkets. The mall is constantly crowded, but the fantastic bargains and wide selection of goods make up for it. Almost anything you require can be found here for a fair price.

The Little India Arcade is the best spot to shop for traditional Indian apparel. Numerous stores and shops that sell sarees, salwar kameez, and other traditional Indian clothing can be found in this covered arcade. A excellent place to buy souvenirs including jewelry, handmade goods, and original artwork is the arcade.

Go to the Tekka Centre for a more genuine experience. Locals love this crowded market because of the fresh food, spices, and street cuisine it offers. Ghee and mangoes are only two examples of the typical Indian ingredients that may be found here. Along with your food, you can find a deal in the market's department for clothing, textiles, and accessories.

The Serangoon Road district is yet another essential Little India retail location. Several stores selling gold jewelry, precious stones, and delicate handcrafted goods are located here. The family-owned stores here have been in operation for many decades and offer one-of-a-kind, genuine items that are difficult to locate elsewhere.

Activities

In the center of Singapore, there is a bustling and colorful district called Little India. This region is a center for Indian culture and cuisine and is home to a sizable population of Indian migrants. Little India is the place to go if you want an authentic Indian experience. The best things to do in Little India are listed below.

Visit the Sri Veeramakaliamman Temple, one of Singapore's most important and historic Hindu temples. It is famed for its magnificent architecture and deft carvings and is devoted to the goddess Kali. The temple is open for tours, where guests can learn about Hinduism and its customs.

Discover the Mustafa Centre: This enormous shopping complex is a favorite of both locals and visitors and is open around-the-clock. Everything is for sale there, including clothes, jewelry, spices, and electronics. It's simple for visitors to lose hours perusing the endless aisles of goods.

Enjoy some Indian food: With so many Indian restaurants and food booths, Little India is a foodie's heaven. Try delicacies like dosas, biryani, and butter chicken, which are all well-liked. Little India offers wonderful, reasonably priced food.

Attend a cultural event: Little India holds a number of cultural events all year long, including Thaipusam and Diwali. The neighborhood comes alive during these festivities with vibrant decorations, ethnic music, and dance performances. Visitors can become fully immersed in Indian culture and discover the local community's traditions and customs.

Shop for ethnic apparel and textiles: Little India is renowned for its textile stores, which provide a variety of materials, from silk and cotton to elaborate embroidery and beaded. Additionally, tourists can discover stunning traditional Indian apparel like sarees and salwar kameez for reasonable costs.

SINGAPORE ZOO

Sight

A well-known tourist destination in the world, the Singapore Zoo is home to more than 2,800 animals from more than 300 different kinds. Visitors can anticipate seeing a wide variety of animals, from well-known species like orangutans and giant pandas to endangered species like the white rhinoceros. The zoo, which has a large collection of animals, also provides a variety of exhibitions, performances, and activities that are ideal for families, animal enthusiasts, and anybody seeking a special and unforgettable experience.

The Primate Kingdom, one of the most well-liked attractions at the Singapore Zoo, is home to an excellent array of primates, including lemurs, chimpanzees, and orangutans from Borneo and Sumatra. In their realistic homes, visitors may observe these active and intelligent animals swinging, climbing, and interacting with one another. Another exhibit not to be missed is the Great Rift Valley of Ethiopia, which showcases a variety of animals from the African savannah, including lions, zebras, and giraffes.

The Rainforest Kidzworld, a portion of the Singapore Zoo specifically created for kids, is another highlight. This area offers pony rides, a petting zoo, a water play area, and even a small train that tours the zoo. Another well-liked attraction is the Splash

Safari Show, where guests can see trained dolphins and sea lions do incredible tricks and stunts.

The Singapore Zoo's Night Safari is one of its most distinctive attractions, allowing guests to wander the grounds after sundown and observe nocturnal creatures including bats, civets, and hyenas. Visitors have the option of taking a guided tram ride or going on a walking tour to get up close to the animals, and the zoo is filled with unique lighting to create a spooky and wonderful ambiance.

The Singapore Zoo is a fantastic location that provides a variety of fun and instructive activities for visitors of all ages. The zoo is a must-see sight for anybody traveling to Singapore because of its sizable variety of animals, immersive exhibits, and interactive activities.

Eating

The Singapore Zoo is renowned for its distinctive and immersive wildlife encounters, but it also offers a variety of eating options to suit the tastes of tourists. The zoo has a number of restaurants that serve a variety of foods, from regional specialties to far-flung cuisines, all with a hint of Singaporean flair.

Ah Meng Restaurant is one of the preferred dining establishments at the Singapore Zoo. The restaurant serves a variety of regional and Asian dishes, including curry fish head, laksa, and hainanese chicken rice. The Ah Meng Restaurant is named for Ah Meng, a well-known orangutan who once lived in the zoo and was a star. It offers outside eating where guests may savor their meal amidst beautiful vegetation and the sounds of the animals.

The zoo also offers the unique experience of Jungle Breakfast with Wildlife, where guests can eat breakfast in the company of amiable orangutans and other animals. International breakfast staples like bacon, sausages, eggs, and pancakes are offered at the buffet, along with regional favorites like nasi lemak, roti prata, and mee siam.

There are a number of fast food restaurants, including KFC, McDonald's, and Subway. The eateries serve traditional fast-food staples like burgers, fries, and fried chicken.

The zoo offers vegetarian and vegan options as well. The Pavilion Vegetarian Café offers vegetarian fare such tofu burgers, vegetarian laksa, and vegetarian bee hoon.

Additionally, the zoo has a number of kiosks and cafes, including ice cream stalls and coffee shops, where visitors can purchase food and beverages.

Overall, a variety of meal alternatives that accommodate different dietary preferences are offered to guests of the Singapore Zoo. The zoo offers something for everyone, whether tourists are searching for a quick snack or a full-fledged dining experience.

Drinking

A distinctive experience that lets tourists quench their thirst while taking in the beauties of wildlife is drinking at the Singapore Zoo. The zoo offers a variety of beverages, from bottled water to freshly squeezed juices, to suit all tastes and dietary needs.

The Lemongrass drink is one of the most well-liked alcoholic beverages in Singapore Zoo. Freshly crushed lemongrass stalks are used to make this aromatic, cooling beverage, which is ideal for hot, muggy days. Visitors can also sip on a variety of freshly squeezed fruit juices, including orange, apple, and watermelon, which are loaded with vital vitamins and minerals.

There are several milkshake options available for those who would want something a little more decadent. These rich, creamy desserts come in flavors like strawberry, chocolate, and vanilla and are excellent for cooling off on a hot day.

Singapore Zoo offers a number of water coolers throughout the park in addition to refreshments. These coolers are a terrific method to rehydrate during the day and fill up on water. Reusable water bottles are encouraged for visitors, since they not only help to decrease plastic waste but also help them save money on beverages.

The rigorous no-alcohol restriction of Singapore Zoo should be noted. This is in keeping with the zoo's goal to encourage ethical and sustainable travel. The policy is in place in order to protect both the welfare of the animals and the visitors.

Activities

With over 2,800 animals from 300 species, the Singapore Zoo, also known as the Mandai Zoo, is a well-known tourist destination that provides tourists with a distinctive and fascinating experience. The zoo offers a variety of events that are suitable for guests of all ages and interests.

The animal presentations at the Singapore Zoo are among the most well-liked events. At various points throughout the zoo, visitors can witness the daily shows, which include various creatures like orangutans, sea lions, and elephants. Visitors can learn about the characteristics and skills of the animals while being entertained at these shows. At designated locations, visitors can also interact with some of the animals, such as feeding giraffes or up close and personal with lemurs.

The Night Safari at the Singapore Zoo is another thrilling experience that lets guests tour the zoo after hours and witness nocturnal animals in their natural settings. Visitors to the Night Safari are taken on a guided tram ride through seven different geographic areas, each of which features a distinctive wildlife habitat. The walking pathways offer visitors the chance to explore on foot while seeing wildlife including spotted hyenas, binturongs, and pangolins.

Visitors can choose the Jungle Breakfast with Wildlife for a more immersive experience, where they can eat in the company of orangutans and other creatures. This is a rare chance to go close to the animals and even snap pictures with them.

Additionally, the Singapore Zoo provides a variety of behind-the-scenes excursions that let visitors understand more about the zoo's management and animal care. The Rainforest Fights Back Tour teaches visitors about the zoo's conservation initiatives and how they can help protect the rainforest, while the Wild Discoverer Tour takes them behind the scenes to observe how the animals are fed and cared for.

CLARKE QUAY

Sight

One of Singapore's most well-known and energetic neighborhoods is Clarke Quay, which is situated in the middle of the city. This seaside neighborhood is renowned for its wide variety of eateries, pubs, and clubs that welcome both locals and visitors. In addition to its fantastic food and entertainment options, Clarke Quay is home to a number of sites that give tourists a window into the city's rich history and culture.

The Singapore River, which runs right down the center of Clarke Quay, is one of the neighborhood's most recognizable landmarks. Visitors can take a beautiful river cruise along the Singapore River to view the city's skyline, learn about the city's colonial past, and marvel at the old shophouses that line the riverbanks. For a more hands-on experience, tourists can also rent a paddleboat or kayak and paddle their way down the river.

Several museums that give insight into the city's cultural legacy are also located in Clarke Quay. With its extensive collection of artifacts and displays exhibiting the region's many art and traditions, the Asian Civilizations Museum is a must-visit for anybody interested in the history and culture of Asia. Another must-see is the Singapore Art Museum, which houses an extraordinary collection of modern art and design.

Clarke Quay offers a number of adrenaline-pumping activities for those looking for a more intense experience. Visitors have the opportunity to experience a heart-stopping adrenaline rush as they are launched into the air at breakneck speed with the G-Max Reverse Bungy, which is a must-try. Another thrilling ride that is not for the faint of heart is the GX-5 Extreme Swing, which sends riders hurtling into the air at incredible speeds.

In general, Clarke Quay is a thriving and fascinating neighborhood that has something to offer everyone. Clarke Quay will not disappoint, whether you're searching for a relaxing river cruise, a cultural experience, or an adrenaline-pumping adventure.

Eating

Singapore's Clarke Quay is a bustling and well-liked tourist and local magnet. For foodies eager to experience the best cuisines from across the world, Clarke Quay is a must-visit site. It is well known for its lively environment, breathtaking waterfront vistas, and a vast variety of dining alternatives.

The wide variety of cuisines offered is one of the best things about dining in Clarke Quay. A variety of cuisines, including Chinese, Japanese, Indian, Italian, and more, are available to visitors. Everyone may find a place to eat, from exclusive fine dining establishments to more relaxed eateries.

Jumbo Seafood at Clarke Quay is a must-visit for seafood lovers. They feature various seafood selections such prawns, fish, and lobster in addition to their well-known Chilli Crab dish, which is a crowd favorite. Visit the Sushi Tei for their famous Dragon Roll, which is created with eel, cucumber, and avocado, if you're in the mood for sushi.

The Clarke Quay Food Street offers a range of regional specialties like Hainanese chicken rice, satay, and laksa for visitors seeking a genuine Singaporean experience.

The costs are reasonable, making this a fantastic choice for individuals on a tight budget.

The Riverhouse offers a classier dining experience with modern Chinese food in a refined and elegant setting. Additionally, the restaurant provides breathtaking views of the Singapore River and the surrounding area.

Along with the food, Clarke Quay provides a vibrant ambiance with a wide variety of entertainment alternatives. Live music performances, street performances, and a variety of taverns and clubs are all available to visitors.

For anyone wishing to indulge in a range of delectable cuisines while taking in the lively environment and breathtaking waterfront views, dining in Clarke Quay is a fantastic experience overall.

Drinking

The core business center of Singapore's Clarke Quay is a thriving nightlife district known for its diverse selection of bars and clubs. There are several places to drink on Clarke Quay, ranging from traditional pubs to hip rooftop bars, each with its own distinct atmosphere and vibe.

The Pump Room is a great option for those seeking a more conventional pub experience. This venue is well-known for both its live music events and its distinctive house-brewed beers. The layout of the pub makes it possible for customers to take in the lively atmosphere while drinking a cold beer.

Another well-liked place to get drunk in Clarke Quay is the multi-level club Attica, which is well-known for its exciting DJ performances and distinctive themed events. Both locals and visitors come to this club to enjoy the energizing music and dance floor, making up a broad clientele.

The Highlander Bar & Restaurant offers a welcoming atmosphere with a large selection of beers, whiskeys, and other spirits if you're looking for something a little more laid-back. The bar features a typical Scottish style with wooden furnishings, complete with kilts and bagpipes.

There are various rooftop bars at Clarke Quay, including Level Up and Altimate, for those who prefer to enjoy their drinks while taking in the scenery. After a long day of sightseeing, these pubs are the ideal spot to rest because they provide breathtaking views of the Singapore cityscape.

Activities

In Singapore, Clarke Quay is a well-liked tourist area that provides a wide range of activities for its guests. Clarke Quay, which is situated along the Singapore River, offers a distinctive fusion of food, entertainment, and nightlife options that are ideal for anyone looking to have a good time.

A river tour is among the most well-liked activities at Clarke Quay. Take a picturesque tour along the Singapore River by boarding one of the many boats that leave from Clarke Quay. This is a fantastic way to see some of the Marina Bay Sands hotel and the Merlion monument, two of the city's most well-known sights.

Dining is another well-liked pastime at Clarke Quay. The region is home to a huge number of eateries and food stands that provide a wide variety of cuisines, from traditional Singaporean fare to global favorites. The lively ambiance and breathtaking river views can be enjoyed while dining.

Clarke Quay offers a wide variety of nightlife choices for those who are interested. Due to the area's abundance of pubs and nightclubs, it is well-liked among partygoers. While consuming beverages and listening to live music, guests can dance the night away.

Visitors can browse the numerous stores and boutiques scattered across Clarke Quay for a more leisurely activity. There is something for everyone, from clothing to mementos. The rich cultural past of Singapore is also showcased at a number of art galleries and museums.

Overall, Clarke Quay is a lively and fascinating location that provides tourists with a variety of things to do. In this lively part of Singapore, there is something for everyone, whether you're searching for excitement or relaxation.

MERLION PARK

Sights

The Merlion is a legendary creature with the head of a lion and the body of a fish, and Merlion Park in Singapore is well-known for its iconic monument of the Merlion. The park's breathtaking views of the Marina Bay skyline and the Singapore Flyer, one of the tallest Ferris wheels in the world, are among its key draws. Merlion Park offers visitors a panoramic perspective of some of Singapore's most well-known monuments, making for an absolutely breathtaking sightseeing experience.

The 8.6-meter-tall, 70-ton Merlion monument is a magnificent sight to behold. The monument is perched on a platform overlooking Marina Bay and shoots water into the bay from its mouth, creating a captivating picture. With fine features on the mane and scales of the fish body, the statue is constructed of concrete and painted white. Visitors can capture lifelong memories by taking pictures with the Merlion monument in the background.

The Marina Bay Sands Hotel, one of Singapore's most opulent and recognizable structures, is also visible from the park and provides breathtaking views of it. Three buildings that are connected by a sizable rooftop with an infinity pool and observation deck make up the hotel's distinctive architecture. From a distance, visitors to Merlion Park can view the hotel's rooftop and towers, which is a wonderfully spectacular picture.

The Singapore Flyer, one of the biggest Ferris wheels in the world, can also be seen clearly from the park. The 30-minute journey on the Singapore Flyer, which has a height of 165 meters, offers passengers a breathtaking vantage point of the city. Visitors may see the cabins of the Singapore Flyer revolving high above the city when viewing it from Merlion Park, which is a very amazing sight.

Eating

Singapore's Merlion Park is a well-liked tourist destination and is well-known for its iconic statue of the Merlion, a legendary animal. Although the park is primarily a tourist attraction, there are a number of food establishments nearby that serve both locals and tourists.

Makansutra Gluttons Bay is one of Merlion Park's most well-liked restaurants. Satay, laksa, and chili crab are just a few of the native street foods available at this outdoor food court. It's a nice place to get a quick snack and take in the view of Marina Bay and the Merlion monument because of the laid-back vibe.

The Clifford Pier, a rooftop bar and restaurant of the Fullerton Bay Hotel, offers breathtaking views of the city skyline and the water for those seeking a more sophisticated dining experience. With items like miso-glazed cod and wagyu beef burgers, the menu combines Asian and Western cuisine. It's the ideal location for a special event or a romantic evening.

The Singapore River Cruise, which provides a dining experience on a boat while it travels along the Singapore River, is an additional choice for foodies at Merlion Park. A range of foods, including seafood specialties and international cuisine, are available on the menu. For those who wish to eat while taking in the city skyline and lights, the experience is ideal.

Last but not least, guests can go to Satay by the Bay, which is close to Merlion Park. In addition to a variety of local street food alternatives, this outdoor food court also has vegetarian and halal selections. The satay, which is barbecued over an open flame and topped with peanut sauce, is the menu's star item.

Overall, Merlion Park and the surrounding area provide a wide variety of dining establishments. Visitors can find cuisine to fit their taste and budget while taking in the stunning city views, from street food to gourmet restaurants.

Drinking

In the center of Singapore, Merlion Park is a well-liked tourist site that is well-known for its distinctive Merlion statue and breathtaking waterfront vistas. Many visitors to the park stop by to take pictures and take in the view, but others might also be interested in getting a drink or two to sip as they take it all in.

Depending on your interests and price range, Merlion Park offers a variety of drinking options. There are also nearby hawker centers and food stalls where you can have a cold beer or a refreshing beverage to sip while you explore the park if you're seeking for a more laid-back experience.

There are various bars and restaurants in the vicinity that provide a variety of drinks and cocktails if you'd prefer a more premium experience. For instance, the Fullerton Bay Hotel, which is close to the park, has a rooftop bar with magnificent views of the Singapore cityscape and a broad selection of drinks.

When drinking in Merlion Park, it's important to remember that Singapore has severe regulations prohibiting intoxication in public places. Between 10:30 p.m. and 7 a.m., it is against the law to consume alcohol in public areas, and offenders may be subject to harsh fines or even jail time.

Overall, as long as you behave sensibly and within the rules, drinking in Merlion Park can be a joyful and delightful experience. There are many choices to fit your tastes and budget, whether you prefer a casual beer or a costly cocktail. Just be mindful of the passing time and refrain from overindulging so that you can enjoy your time in the park in a responsible and safe manner.

Activities

The Merlion statue, a hybrid of a lion and a fish, is the centerpiece of Merlion Park, a well-liked tourist destination in Singapore. Merlion Park offers guests a variety of things to do besides take pictures with the Merlion.

A picturesque river ride down the Singapore River is among the best things to do at Merlion Park. The Fullerton Hotel, Clarke Quay, and the Esplanade are just a few of the historical sites that may be seen while taking in the city's skyline from the river cruise. A guided tour of the river's history and architecture is available on a variety of river cruises, including daytime and evening cruises.

The Merlion Walk, a promenade that runs alongside Marina Bay's waterfront, is another well-liked activity. The Marina Bay Sands, the Singapore Flyer, and the city skyline are all magnificently visible from The Merlion Walk, which is the ideal location for a leisurely stroll. Along the promenade, there are sculptures and other pieces of art that enhance the area's creative atmosphere.

Along with soaking in the views and sounds of the neighborhood, visitors can also enjoy a picnic in the park. Visitors can enjoy regional street food from neighboring food carts, and Merlion Park offers various grassy spots ideal for a picnic.

The Merlion Park Visitor Center should definitely be visited by anyone interested in learning more about Singapore's past. The Merlion statue's history is one of many exhibitions inside the Visitor Center that highlight Singapore's history and culture.

JURONG BIRD PARK

Sights

One of Singapore's most well-known attractions, Jurong Bird Park draws visitors from all over the world who are interested in birds and the natural world. It is the largest bird park in Asia and is home to many different avian species from over the world, with over 5,000 birds representing 400 different species. The following are some of the attractions in Jurong Bird Park:

The 30-meter-high waterfall in the largest walk-in aviary in the world, the Waterfall Aviary, is home to over 600 free-flying birds, including the stunning and critically endangered Bali Mynah.

Six different kinds of penguins, including the king penguin and the rockhopper penguin, may be found at the Penguin Coast exhibit, which also includes a reproduction of their natural habitat, complete with snowy cliffs and a 3D movie.

Thousands of vibrant and sociable lorikeets can be fed and petted in the enormous aviary known as the Lory Loft. While strolling around the aviary, visitors can purchase a cup of nectar and hand-feed the birds.

Pelican Cove: The endangered Dalmatian Pelican is one of the several types of pelicans that call Pelican Cove home. Visitors can engage with them while they are feeding, watch them swim, and observe them fly.

African birds like the magnificent Violet Turaco and the African Grey Hornbill are housed at the African Waterfall Aviary, a sizable aviary. A stunning waterfall and a fake African rainforest are among features of the aviary.

The greater flamingo, one of the most recognizable and stunning birds in the world, calls Flamingo Lake home. In their natural habitat, which includes a lovely lake surrounded by thick vegetation, visitors may observe the flamingos strutting and feeding.

For everyone interested in environment and wildlife, Jurong Bird Park is a fascinating and informative experience. Anyone visiting Singapore should go there; it's a terrific place to spend the day with family and friends.

Eating

A well-liked tourist destination in Singapore, Jurong Bird Park provides a special chance to enjoy nature and get up close to the lovely bird species. 400 different species of birds totaling over 5,000 make for a memorable experience for tourists.

The park's eating selections are one of its best features. Visitors can select from a wide range of eateries and cafes, each of which offers a distinctive gastronomic experience. One well-liked location is the family-friendly eatery Birdz of Play, which provides delectable regional food. The restaurant offers a kid-friendly outdoor playground, making it a great place for families to dine out while their little ones play.

The Hawk Cafe, which is next to the Hawk Arena, is yet another fantastic dining choice. Visitors can eat here and observe raptor birds of prey practicing their hunting techniques. Japanese, Italian, and native

Singaporean cuisines are among the many international cuisines offered at the cafe.

There are various kiosks and snack stalls dotted around the park for visitors looking for a quick bite. These provide a selection of food, including beverages, popcorn, and ice cream. A sandwich or a salad can also be purchased at the Birdz & Wormz kiosk, which is close to Flamingo Lake.

Overall, dining in Jurong Bird Park is a distinctive experience that caters to all tastes. The park's varied food options have you covered whether you're searching for a kid-friendly eatery, a spectacular dining experience, or a fast snack. Therefore, Jurong Bird Park is the ideal destination if you're planning a trip to Singapore and want to savor delicious food while taking in the splendor of nature.

Drinking

Visitors enjoy having drinks at Jurong Bird Park, particularly on hot, muggy days. Water, soft drinks, and alcoholic beverages are among the selection of refreshments that the park serves at various locations. These beverages are available for purchase at restaurants, vending machines, and kiosks.

While it is permitted to drink in Jurong Bird Park, visitors must follow the rules and policies of the facility. Visitors under the age of 18 are strictly barred from consuming alcohol. Additionally, guests are not permitted to enter the park with their own alcoholic beverages.

Alcoholic beverages must be purchased at the specified parks places for use by visitors. Beer, wine, and cocktails are among the alcoholic beverages that are offered. Drinks can be enjoyed by visitors in approved areas like the Flamingo Lake or the Birdz of Play playground.

It's vital to remember that guests who drink alcohol are accountable for their own actions and must refrain from any conduct that could damage others or themselves. Visitors who are intoxicated will be asked to leave the park.

The park provides a selection of non-alcoholic drinks in addition to alcoholic ones to help visitors stay hydrated while they are there. A number of places have water coolers, and kiosks and restaurants sell bottled water, soft drinks, and juices to patrons.

Activities

A renowned bird sanctuary with about 20.2 hectares of lush vegetation, Jurong Bird Park is situated in Singapore. One of the largest bird parks in the world, the park is home to approximately 5,000 birds from 400 different species. The park offers a variety of activities to keep visitors interested and amused and is a must-visit location for bird watchers and environmental enthusiasts alike.

The Birds of Prey presentation is among Jurong Bird Park's most well-liked attractions. Awe-inspiring aerial acrobatics performed by majestic birds like eagles, hawks, and falcons are on display in this show. The presentation is instructive as well as entertaining, with trainers describing the traits and behavior of the birds as they do amazing aerial tricks.

The Penguin Coast exhibit, which is home to numerous kinds of penguins, including the endangered African penguin, is another well-liked feature of Jurong Bird Park. In order to get up close and personal with these gorgeous birds, visitors can participate in a feeding session as well as watch the penguins swim and play in their natural environment.

The Lory Loft is a must-see site for anyone who enjoys interacting with birds. Visitors can feed the over 1,000 multicolored lorikeets that live in this exhibit nectar while they perch on their arms. The encounter is certainly one-of-a-kind, and guests can take some priceless photos with the birds.

The Flamingo Lake, where guests may observe the magnificent pink flamingos in their natural habitat, and the Pelican Cove, which is home to various species of pelicans, are only two of the additional activities available at Jurong Bird Park. A tram ride throughout the park allows visitors to view the numerous displays and activities.

Chapter 4

Day Trip from Singapore

Desaru

Desaru is among the top locations for quick

trips from Singapore and is ideal for weekend excursions. This location is the ideal get-away from the hectic pace of city life because of its laid-back atmosphere and sandy beaches. One of the best locations to visit in Malaysia is an underappreciated island with white sand beaches and clear waters that have a calming effect on a worried mind. From Changi Ferry Terminal, this location with its spectacular fruit farms and upscale golf courses is only accessible by ferry.

As they have fantastic golf sessions to offer for both serious golfers and beginners, this location is a golfer's heaven. The 'excellent' season to visit this location is from April to October, however June to August is when it gets the busiest. Adventure lovers may like activities like snorkeling and surfing.

Location: Malaysia

Best Time To Visit: April to October

How to reach: Take a ferry from Changi Ferry Terminal

Places To Eat: 261 Bar Restaurant, Desaru Coast Riverside, and Nelayan Seafood By The Coast

Where To Stay: Hard Rock Hotel, The Westin Desaru Coast Resort, and Lotus Desaru Beach Resort & Spa

Tourist Attractions: Desaru Beach, Adventure Waterpark, and Desaru Fruit Farm

Cameron Highlands

Singapore's Cameron Highlands This location is a nine-hour coach ride from Singapore if you're thinking about taking a quick getaway. Even while it may sound exhausting, it's worth it to visit this wonderful location, which allows you to experience the coolest temperatures without flying halfway across the world. This location is well known for its strawberries and large tea estates, making it a fantastic family destination. In Cameron Highlands, adorable small carts sell mouthwatering burgers that are finger-licking fantastic. If you're searching for something longer than a weekend escape, this is the ideal 3-day short trip from Singapore. You can even combine it with skydiving in Malaysia.

Your passion for plants should compel you to visit this gorgeous lavender garden, which offers a wide range of products created from the herb as well as information on its therapeutic and medicinal benefits. Mossy Forest, Parit Waterfall, Robinson Waterfall, Time Tunnel, the Local Museum, and Butterfly Garden are further Cameron Highland tourist sites that are ideal day trips from Singapore.

Location: Malaysia
Best Time To Visit: Throughout the year
How to reach: Hire a taxi
Places To Eat: Cactus View Restaurant, May Flower Restaurant, and Delicious & Happiness Kitchen
Where To Stay: Kea Garden Guest House, The Lake House, and Century Pines Resort
Tourist Attractions: Time Tunnel and Cameron Tringkap Bee Farm

Malacca

Malacca is the place to go if you want to take a quick journey outside of Singapore. A short journey from Singapore will take you to this attractive and serene location, which is only a few hours from the border. What this area offers guests is a beautiful change of scenery. Hundreds of stores and vendors weave through the charming and lovely medieval lanes, further enhancing the area's splendor. This lovely town would be ideal for anyone seeking a quick getaway from Singapore with loved ones or as a couple; read the Malaysia travel guide to learn more!

Some of the island's attractions include tea establishments where you may learn the "proper" way to drink tea and a house-turned-museum where you can see local culture. Additionally, this island has several nice attributes like wonderful food and antiques. When visiting Malacca, you absolutely must try the tandoori chicken and several curries. Christ Church, Dutch Square, the Malaysian Navy Museum,

Cheng Hoon Teng Temple, and the Baba and Nyonya Peranakan Museum are a few of the heritage sites that are regularly visited by tourists.

Location: Malaysia
Best Time To Visit: April and May
How to reach: Nearest railhead is Pulau Sebang
Places To Eat: Nancy's Kitchen, The Baboon House, and Low Yong Moh Restaurant
Where To Stay: Hatten Hotel, DoubleTree by Hilton, and Rosa Malacca
Tourist Attractions: A Famosa, Christ Church, Stadthuys, and Church of St. Paul

Penang

Penang should be on your list of weekend getaways from Singapore if you're looking for destinations that are close by and easy to get to from Singapore. The center of arts and culture is in Penang. You will undoubtedly be impressed by the vibrant streets. In addition, it is renowned for its hawker fare. Be sure to sample the cuisine, and don't forget to visit the best Penang beaches, such as Tanjung Bungah and Batu Ferringhi. Penang is unquestionably one of the nicest locations close to Singapore because of its lively atmosphere.

Location: Malaysia

Best Time To Visit: November to February

How to reach: Take a train from Kuala Lumpur.

Places To Eat: Markus Restaurant, Orinea, and Sushi Kitchen Gurney Plaza

Where To Stay: 1926 Heritage Hotel, The Gurney Resort, and Berjaya Penang Hotel

Tourist Attractions: Penang Hill, Gurney Drive, and Kek Lok Si Temple.

Genting Highlands

In Malaysia's Pahang region is the integrated resort community of Genting

Highlands. Hotels, eateries, shopping centers including SkyAvenue Mall and Genting Premium Outlets, casinos, and theme parks are all present there. One of the best tourist destinations that can be visited on a quick trip from Singapore is located at a height of 1,740 meters on the Titiwangsa Mountains. Enjoy the thrilling Cable Card trip, too. Genting Highlands is unquestionably one of the best locations nearby Singapore due to the abundance of recreational opportunities.

Location: Malaysia

Best Time To Visit: March to September

How to reach: Take a bus or hire a taxi

Places To Eat: Coffee Terrace, Burger & Lobster Malaysia, and Restaurant Loong Kee

Where To Stay: First World Hotel, Grand Ion Delemen Hotel, and Theme Park Hotel

Tourist Attractions: Casino De Genting, Snow World, and Chin Swee Caves Temple

Sentosa Highland

It is one of the Singaporean cities that is most nearby and one of the nearest travel destinations. It is unquestionably the best short vacation to take from Singapore. One of the most outstanding tourist destinations in Singapore is the island of Sentosa, which has a number of amusement parks, beaches, and the world-famous Universal Studios Singapore theme park and water park.

Location: Singapore

Best time to visit: June- July, October – December

How to reach: Take the Singapore MRT Service. From Harbourfront Station, enter VivoCity Mall. Go to the third floor (Level 3)

of VivoCity Mall. Purchase a Sentosa Pass. Board the Sentosa Express.

Places To Eat: Malaysian Food Street, Ocean Restaurant, Din Tai Fung Resort

Where To Stay: Harbour Ville Hotel, Siloso Beach Resort, and Travelodge Harbourfront

Tourist Attractions: Universal Studios, Gardens by the Bay, and Sands Expo

Chapter 5

Practical Information for Travelers

Accessible Travel

Southeast Asian city-state Singapore is well-known for its pristine streets, effective public transportation, and thriving cultural scene. It is a highly developed metropolis. Singapore has made a big effort to make sure that visitors with disabilities or limited mobility may also enjoy the city's various attractions because of its commitment to accessibility and inclusivity.

With all buses and trains having ramps, priority seating, and obvious signage, the city has made tremendous strides in accessibility. For the benefit of passengers who are blind or visually impaired, the Mass Rapid Transit (MRT) system has additionally installed tactile flooring, braille signage, and audio announcements. For people with impairments who need door-to-door transportation, the Land Transport Authority now offers a special Dial-A-Ride service.

Hotels in Singapore have worked to accommodate visitors with disabilities. Many hotels provide accessible rooms with amenities like roll-in showers, grab bars, and doors that are suitable for wheelchairs. On demand, some hotels additionally offer specialized tools like hoists or shower chairs.

Major sites in Singapore, including the Marina Bay Sands, Gardens by the Bay, and the Singapore Zoo, include accessible features as well. For guests with disabilities, these attractions offer wheelchair rentals as well as accessible routes, ramps, and lifts. For those with mobility challenges, the Singapore Zoo even provides a free wheelchair service where they can ask for a push assistant to help them navigate the grounds.

Many restaurants in Singapore have wheelchair-friendly entrances, and some offer menus in braille or large print for people looking for accessible dining options.

Additionally, the nation's open-air food courts known as Hawker Centres provide a broad variety of inexpensive and convenient dining options.

In conclusion, Singapore is a city-state dedicated to inclusivity and accessibility. All of the city's dining establishments, hotels, attractions, and public transportation are accessible to people with impairments or restricted mobility. With these safeguards in place, Singapore is a great choice for tourists looking for a warm and convenient travel experience.

Customs Regulations

Singapore is a flourishing, multiethnic city-state with a thriving port and strong economy. To protect its population, economy, and environment, the nation has strong customs restrictions in effect. To avoid any legal issues, it is crucial to comprehend Singapore's customs regulations whether you are a tourist or a businessperson.

First of all, you must disclose any products, cash, or jewels you are bringing into Singapore that are worth more than SGD 30,000 (about USD 22,000). If you don't, you risk fines, jail time, or both. Additionally, you are not permitted to bring in any prohibited objects including illegal narcotics, weapons, counterfeit goods, or pornographic materials. Furthermore, no fruits, vegetables, or meat products may be imported without first receiving authorization from the Agri-Food and Veterinary Authority (AVA). This is done to stop the spread of diseases and pests that could hurt Singapore's agricultural sector.

Secondly, you are not permitted to export any restricted goods like weapons, ammo, explosives, or drugs when you leave Singapore. Additionally, if you are taking money out of Singapore that is more than

SGD 20,000 (about USD 15,000), you must declare it.

Thirdly, you must follow Singapore's rules for customs clearance if you are a businessperson importing or exporting items. For some things like chemicals, plants, or animals, you need to have the right permits and licenses. You must also pay any taxes, tariffs, or other charges that may be associated with your imported or exported items.

Finally, it is significant to remember that any person, luggage, or cargo arriving at or departing from Singapore may be inspected by customs agents. This is done to ensure compliance with customs laws and to stop the smuggling of illegal goods.

In conclusion, Singapore has strict customs laws in place to protect its people, its economy, and the environment. To stay out of legal problems, it's crucial for visitors and businesspeople to be aware of and abide by these rules.

Electricity

A secure and sustainable energy supply is a priority in Singapore's highly developed and dependable electrical sector. The majority of the nation's electricity is produced from natural gas, while solar energy and other renewable energy sources are also becoming more significant.

Senoko Energy, Tuas Power Generation, Keppel Electric, and Sembcorp Industries are the four power generation businesses in Singapore that jointly supply electricity to the nation's power grid. These businesses run a variety of power plants, such as reciprocating engine, steam turbine, and gas-fired combined cycle facilities.
The nation also has ambitions to employ more renewable energy, with a goal of producing 2 gigawatts or more of solar energy by 2030. In order to promote the

growth of renewable energy, the government has launched a number of programs, including the installation of solar panels on public housing complexes and the implementation of a solar leasing program for enterprises.

In addition to its capacity for energy production, Singapore has a well-established electricity system that guarantees consistent electricity delivery throughout the nation. The transmission and distribution networks are run and maintained by SP Group, which also manages the grid.

The government has launched a number of programs to encourage enterprises to adopt energy-efficient practices, such as the Energy Efficiency National Partnership program. A carbon price on greenhouse gas emissions from the electricity industry has also been established in the nation, encouraging businesses to lower their emissions.

In order to meet the nation's energy needs in a sustainable way, Singapore's power industry is a well-developed and dependable system that is constantly improving.

Emergency numbers

Singapore's emergency response system is well-known for being among the best in the world and has been in place for many years. In Singapore, the ambulance emergency number is 995, the police emergency number is 999, and the Singapore Civil Defence Force (SCDF) emergency number is 998.

Emergency Medical Services (EMS), the Singapore Police Force (SPF), and the SCDF, respectively, run the emergency numbers. A qualified operator will take the call when someone dials one of these lines, and they will then ask the caller a series of questions to ascertain the type and seriousness of the emergency.

The EMS will send an ambulance to the caller's location in case of a medical emergency. Highly skilled paramedics who are prepared to manage a variety of medical crises, from heart attacks to serious accidents, work for the EMS. Additionally, the EMS has a fleet of modern ambulances that can rapidly and safely transport patients to the hospital.

When there is a need for law enforcement, the SPF will send officers to the caller's location. The SPF has a wide range of competencies, from handling minor events to managing large crises, and is in charge of upholding law and order in Singapore.

The SCDF will send a group of firemen and rescue specialists to the caller's location in the event of a civil defense emergency. The

SCDF is in charge of addressing a variety of situations, from fires to natural catastrophes, and has a team of specialists who are well-trained and equipped to handle any emergency situation.

Discount Card

Singapore's Discount Card is a loyalty program that provides cardholders with exclusive discounts and promotions at a variety of Singaporean retailers. It is a fantastic opportunity for both citizens and visitors to the city-state to save money while dining, shopping, and taking part in various activities.

The card offers reductions on a variety of goods and services, including dining, shopping, entertainment, attractions, and excursions, ranging from 5% to 50%. In Singapore, more than a thousand businesses are taking part, including well-known names like McDonald's, KFC, Watsons, and numerous others. It is a handy tool for travelers trying to cut costs because cardholders can get discounts on things like lodging and car rentals.

One merely needs to buy the card, either online or at specific retailers, to become a cardholder. The card can be renewed annually and is good for one year. Additionally, cardholders can accumulate rewards points through their purchases, which can then be used for further savings or coupons.

The card also comes with extra perks, such a smartphone app that lets users track their reward points and easily access the newest discounts and promotions. Additionally, during holiday seasons and special occasions like Chinese New Year, Christmas, and the Singapore Grand Prix, the card offers exclusive deals and discounts.

Overall, the Singapore Discount Card is a great way to take advantage of all that Singapore has to offer while saving money. It is a need for anyone trying to stretch their budget without sacrificing quality or pleasure because to its broad selection of partner shops, exclusive offers, and rewards points system.

Internet Access

Singapore is well known for having one of the most established infrastructures for internet access and for being one of the most connected nations in the world. Singapore, an island nation with a tiny but densely populated population, has significantly invested in information and communication technologies (ICTs) to maintain its status as a major worldwide financial and business center. As a result, a significant section of the population now has access to high-speed internet, and consumers have a variety of options to select from.

The Singaporean government's dedication to creating a "Smart Nation" is one of the major forces behind the city-state's internet infrastructure. This program intends to employ technology to raise Singaporeans' quality of life and increase the nation's economic competitiveness. The government has made significant investments in creating a strong digital infrastructure, which includes high-speed broadband networks, data centers, and cloud computing services, in order to accomplish this.

The broadband infrastructure in Singapore is one of the best in the world. Over 95% of homes have access to fiber-based broadband services because to the nation's highly developed fiber-optic infrastructure. The network can deliver speeds up to 10Gbps, one of the fastest in the entire globe. As a result, businesses and citizens in Singapore can engage in lag- and buffer-free high-quality video conferencing, online gaming, and other bandwidth-intensive activities.

Singapore provides a variety of different internet access choices, in addition to fiber broadband, including cable, DSL, and wireless broadband. Customers can thus select the internet connection type that best meets their requirements and financial situation. The wireless broadband network in Singapore is likewise very advanced and has a wide area of coverage. This makes it simple for locals and visitors to keep in touch whether traveling by public transportation or taking in the sights.

Singapore has a highly developed internet infrastructure that offers people and companies high-speed, dependable connectivity. Singapore's internet connection is probably going to keep becoming better in the upcoming years given the government's continued commitment to creating a "Smart Nation" and encouraging the development of the digital economy.

Money

The Monetary Authority of Singapore (MAS) issues the Singapore dollar (SGD or $), which is used in Singapore. The Singapore dollar is available in denominations of $2, $5, $10, $50, $100, $1,000, and $10,000 and is divisible into 100 cents. Additionally, coins are offered in the following values: 5, 10, 20, and 50 cents. The MAS, which is in charge of preserving price stability and fostering sustainable economic growth, controls Singapore's currency.

The Singapore dollar is widely accepted throughout the nation, and banks, exchange booths, and ATMs make it simple to find current exchange rates. In addition to being widely recognized, credit and debit cards, as well as cashless payment systems like PayNow and NETS, have grown in popularity recently.

The currency of Singapore is renowned for its strength and stability. It is heavily traded on the international foreign exchange market, and Singapore's solid economic fundamentals, political stability, and responsible monetary policy are credited as contributing to its strength. The Singapore dollar's exchange rate is controlled by the MAS by allowing it to vary within a range when compared to a basket of other currencies. By doing this, the MAS is able to keep prices stable and the exchange rate competitive.

The incorporation of security mechanisms to prevent counterfeiting is one distinctive aspect of Singaporean cash. For instance, the holographic strip and watermark on the $50 and $100 bills make it challenging to counterfeit them. To stay one step ahead of counterfeiters, the MAS also modifies the currency's design on occasion.

Overall, Singapore's currency is a representation of the nation's stability and economic prosperity. Its strength and stability have made it a well-liked currency among traders and investors, and its security features guarantee that it will always be a trusted and safe method of payment for both Singaporeans and foreigners.

Public Holidays

With a varied population that observes a variety of festivals and holidays, Singapore is a multicultural nation. The nation observes a total of eleven public holidays annually. These celebrations are a significant component of Singaporean culture and are essential in bringing the nation's various ethnic groups together.

New Year's Day, which falls on January 1st, is the first holiday of the year. Chinese New Year, a two-day event that ushers in the lunar calendar and typically takes place between January and February, comes next. The majority of Singaporeans of Chinese heritage celebrate this holiday, and the streets are filled with vibrant decorations, lion dances, and fireworks.

Following Labor Day on May 1, which honors workers' contributions to the nation's economy, comes Good Friday, a Christian festival commemorating the crucifixion of Jesus Christ.

Hari Raya Puasa and Hari Raya Haji are two public holidays observed by the Muslim population in Singapore. A one-day celebration called Hari Raya Puasa celebrates the end of Ramadan, while Hari Raya Haji, also known as the Festival of Sacrifice, honors Ibrahim's willingness to offer his son as a sacrifice to Allah.

One of the most important public holidays in Singapore is National Day, which is observed on August 9 and commemorates the year that Singapore gained independence from Malaysia. There are parades, fireworks displays, and cultural performances, as well as red and white decorations all over the streets.

The Hindu community celebrates Deepavali, commonly referred to as the Festival of Lights, which takes place between October and November. The victory of light over darkness is celebrated on this one-day holiday.

Christmas Day and Boxing Day, which are both Christian holidays, are the final two public holidays of the year.

In conclusion, Singapore's public holidays constitute a significant part of its culture and heritage. They facilitate interaction between individuals from various ethnic backgrounds and offer a venue for celebration and introspection. Singaporeans can take advantage of this time off from work and school to spend time with their families and loved ones.

Taxes & Refund

Singapore is renowned for its aggressive tax policies, which have aided in luring foreign company and investment. The nation's tax structure is intended to be straightforward, open, and effective, with low rates and a wide tax base. The taxes and refunds in Singapore are broken out as follows:

Personal Income Tax: Singapore has progressive personal income tax rates that range from 0% to a maximum of 22% for people making over SGD 320,000 annually. However, because of different tax breaks and deductions, the majority of citizens experience lower effective tax rates. For instance, Singapore tax residents are not required to pay taxes on the first SGD 1 million of their income, and they are allowed to deduct things like charitable contributions, home mortgage interest payments, and medical costs.

Corporate Income Tax: Singapore has one of the lowest corporate income tax rates in the world, at a flat 17%. The nation also provides a range of tax breaks and incentives for companies that operate in particular industries or carry out particular activities. For instance, businesses engaged in R&D may qualify for tax deductions of up to 400% of qualifying expenses.

Singapore's GST, or Goods and Services Tax, is a 7% value-added tax imposed on the delivery of goods and services. Residential houses and financial services are two examples of products and services that are exempt from the GST. However, subject to a few restrictions, visitors to Singapore can request a refund of the GST they paid on any purchases they made while they were there.

Owners of both residential and non-residential properties in Singapore must pay property tax. The annual value of the property—which corresponds to the expected annual rental value of the property if it were to be rented out—is the basis for the tax. The tax rates range from 0% to 10%; non-residential properties are subject to higher rates.

Time

Singapore's time zone is Singapore Standard Time (SST), which is 8 hours ahead of Coordinated Universal Time (UTC+8). This time zone was officially introduced by Singapore on January 1st, 1982, replacing the preceding Malayan Standard Time.

Singapore's adoption of SST was primarily motivated by economic and practical factors. Being positioned at the southern tip of the Malay Peninsula, Singapore shares identical geographical coordinates with Malaysia, which is only one hour behind Singapore. However, Singapore's choice to adopt a different time zone was made to coordinate with its neighboring countries in Southeast Asia, such as Indonesia and the Philippines. This alignment provides for improved cooperation and communication across the region.

Singapore's time is not influenced by daylight saving time (DST) adjustments, given the country is positioned near the equator and sees relatively continuous day and night cycles throughout the year. Therefore, Singapore's time remains consistent throughout the year, with no modifications needed.

The Singapore government's dedication to preserving precise time is evidenced through the National Time and Frequency Standard, which is maintained by the

National Metrology Centre (NMC) of the Agency for Science, Technology and Research (A*STAR). This standard assures that all clocks and timepieces in Singapore are synchronized to the same time source, delivering accurate and reliable time information for the nation.

Overall, Singapore's time zone is an important part of the country's infrastructure and plays a critical role in promoting international trade, communication, and transportation. The use of SST has enabled Singapore to synchronize its activities with its regional equivalents, boosting efficiency and production.

Tourist Information

One of the most well-liked tourist destinations in Southeast Asia is Singapore, which has a variety of activities and attractions to suit tourists of all ages and interests. The city-state is well known for its orderliness, effectiveness, and safety, making it the perfect vacation spot for tourists seeking a stress-free getaway.

There are several different ways to find tourist information on Singapore, including brochures, books, and websites. VisitSingapore.com, the city's official tourism website, offers a thorough overview to the city's attractions, lodging alternatives, food establishments, and events. The website also provides a number of tools and information, such as suggested itineraries, maps, and transportation guides, to aid visitors in planning their travels.

The Marina Bay Sands complex, which houses an opulent hotel, a retail center, a casino, and a rooftop infinity pool with breathtaking views of the city skyline, is one of Singapore's most well-known attractions. The Gardens by the Bay, a futuristic park with enormous supertrees, indoor gardens, and a breathtaking light and sound show at night, is another well-liked attraction.

The city's cultural attractions are similarly outstanding, with standouts including the Chinatown Heritage Centre and the National Gallery Singapore, which both hold sizable collections of Southeast Asian art. Visitors can get a taste of Singapore's cuisine by visiting the city's hawker centers, which provide a wide selection of regional foods at reasonable costs.

Singapore has a variety of lodging options to fit all preferences and financial constraints. Visitors can discover lodging options that suit their needs, from five-star hotels to inexpensive hostels. The public transit system in the city is also incredibly effective, making it simple for visitors to travel and take advantage of everything Singapore has to offer.

Ways to save Money

Singapore is renowned for being a thriving city-state, but living there can also be pricey. However, there are a number of methods to save money in Singapore with some preparation and work. Here are some practical strategies for managing your spending and making the most of your money.

Consider using public transportation: Singapore's system is quite effective and reasonably priced. You can regularly save a sizable sum of money by using the bus or MRT instead of a cab.

Cooking at home might help you save money on food because eating out can be pricey in Singapore. You can also save money on groceries by shopping at nearby hawker centers and wet markets.

Use coupons and discount apps: Singaporeans appreciate a good deal, and there are several websites and apps that provide discounts on everything from entertainment to food. Chope, Entertainer, and Fave are a few of the well-liked choices.

If you have a spare room in your house, you might want to think about renting it out to help pay for your living expenses. Finding short-term tenants is simple thanks to websites like Roomorama and Airbnb.

Take advantage of the free events and activities Singapore has to offer, such as its museums, parks, and cultural festivals. If you're looking for a list of free activities and events taking place on the island, visit the website of the National Parks Board.

Shop at thrift stores: You can find affordable clothing, furniture, and household things at thrift stores and second-hand stores. Salvation Army, Goodwill, and ValueMax are a few well-liked alternatives.

Reduce your energy use to lower your utility costs. Singapore's hot and humid climate might result in high electricity bills, but there are ways to do this. Your utility bills can be lowered by taking easy steps like shutting off appliances when not in use and switching to energy-efficient lightbulbs.

In conclusion, it's not necessary to spend a fortune to live in Singapore. You may live comfortably and save money by using the city-state's great public transit system, cooking at home, using discount apps, renting out a spare room, taking advantage of free activities, shopping at thrift stores, and lowering your utility expenses.

Visas

Singapore is an island nation and city-state in Southeast Asia, formally known as the Republic of Singapore. It is a thriving metropolis and a center of the world's finance noted for its dynamic culture, first-rate infrastructure, and extensive history. 63 islands make up the country of Singapore, which is home to more than 5.7 million people.

Visas:

Singapore's visa regulations are very simple, allowing nationals of the majority of nations to enter without a visa for brief periods. It is crucial to remember that visa requirements can change based on the visitor's country of origin, the reason for their trip, and the length of their stay.

Australia, Canada, the United States, and the United Kingdom all permit visa-free stays in Singapore for up to 90 days. However, they must also have a return or onward ticket, as well as a passport that is valid for at least six months past the length of their anticipated stay. Visitors must also provide evidence that they have enough money on hand to meet their expenses throughout their stay.

Before their travel, inhabitants of nations that aren't free from the necessity for visas would need to apply for one. Ordinarily simple, applying for a Singapore visa can be done online or in person at the Singapore embassy or consulate that is closest to you.

The various visas that are offered for Singapore include:

Tourist visa: People who want to travel to Singapore must apply for this sort of visa. Typically, tourist visas are provided for 30 days, with the option of an extra 30 days.

Business Visa: Individuals who want to go to Singapore for professional reasons, such as to attend conferences or meetings, must apply for a business visa. Normally granted for 30 days, business visas can be extended for an additional 30 days.

Work Visa: Foreign nationals who have received an employment offer in Singapore are eligible for work visas. The employee's application for a work visa must be made by the company.

Student Visa: Foreign nationals who want to study in Singapore need a student visa. Before requesting a student visa, a student must be admitted to a reputable school in Singapore.

Permanent Residency: Foreign nationals who have lived and worked in Singapore for at least six months are eligible for permanent residency. In Singapore, permanent residents are free to work, study, and live as they like.

The majority of travelers can enter Singapore without a visa for short-term stays, and the visa system in Singapore is, therefore, rather simple. However, it is crucial to confirm the visa requirements based on the origin country, the intended use of the trip, and the intended length of stay. Visitors are likely to have a wonderful experience in Singapore because it is a stunning country with a rich culture.

Printed in Great Britain
by Amazon

24889103R00126